Hailsham at War
1939-41

Hailsham History Group

Hailsham at War
1939-41

edited by George Farebrother

Falmer
Centre for Continuing Education, University of Sussex
1986

Grateful acknowledgement is made for the financial support given in this publication of Hailsham at War by Mr and Mrs Taylor of the Grenadier Hotel; A. Baker and Son; Green Brothers Ltd; The Sussex Express.

© George Farebrother 1986

Published by the Centre for Continuing Education, University of Sussex

Printed by the University of Sussex Printing Unit

Typeset by Oxford University Computing Service

ISBN 0—904242—29—3

CONTENTS

Introduction. 1

CHAPTER 1: A Small Market Town: Hailsham on the eve of War. . . .5

CHAPTER 2: A Land Sore Troubled: The military situation. 9

CHAPTER 3: If they should come: The defence of Hailsham 30

CHAPTER 4: 'There was a plane and I could see something falling...': The organisation of Civil Defence 49

CHAPTER 5: 'Don't you know there's a war on?': Effects of war-time restrictions 63

CHAPTER 6: A Time to Knit: The civilian war effort 73

CHAPTER 7: Forty Years On: Looking back on the war years 83

Notes and references 90

Abbreviations. 96

Maps and Illustrations

1.	The Hailsham area 1939-40	4
2.	The Final Plan for Operation Sea Lion, September 1940	10
3.	L.D.V. assembles before Church Tower Watch	15
4.	The Home Guard Change of Watch on Church Tower	21
5.	Anti-tank Barrier Remaining at Rickney, November 1979. 'Sharks' or 'Dragons' Teeth'	22
6.	Gun positions at Pevensey Castle	23
7.	Surviving Earthworks from the Pevensey Radar Station	28
8.	Nodal Points in East Sussex	32
9.	The Old Vicarage, Market Street. Sharks Teeth in Front Garden. 1940	35
10.	The Hailsham Nodal Point. October 1941	37
11.	Roads reserved for Military Use and Refuge Crossing Points. May 1940	42

Cover illustration: Jack Roberts, Hailsham Home Guard member, operating the 'Molotov Slinger' invented by Private A. Green.

Introduction

For the people of Hailsham, 1985 was the Year of the Bulldozer. There were extensive roadworks and the heart of the town underwent major surgery as a new shopping precinct was inserted. These changes were the culmination of 25 years of change and development in the town. As buildings fall and memory fades and dies, our links with the past become more tenuous.

By screwing up the imagination we can peel away the accumulated layers of the past 45 years and reveal a close-knit wartime community sharing a common apprehension: not, this time, of bulldozers, but of enemy tanks and field-grey uniforms. For all they knew, the people of Hailsham were about to face war, not in faraway places of which they knew little, but as a very present and savage reality. This publication documents their response to this threat.

The Hailsham History Group has been turning over the debris of the past in order to reveal the realities of the early years of the Second World War. The Group has links with the Hailsham Historical and Natural History Society and with the University of Sussex Centre for Continuing Education. By 1979 it had made an intensive study of the late Victorian and Edwardian town, first under myself and then under Dr Short of Sussex University. The fruits of this study, edited by Dr Short, were realised with the publication of 'The String Town'. The Group wished to continue its work on local history and a start was made on a study of the war years in Hailsham.

This publication will almost certainly be of interest to the older people of Hailsham who lived through the war years as well as to younger residents who might feel some curiosity about the period. It is offered to a wider audience as a serious study of a rather neglected area—the response of a small town to the pressures of war. We have enjoyed the challenge of trading off 'hard' sources such as the Civil Defence incident books against 'soft' sources such as personal testimony and newspaper accounts. The truth about the war years, as far as we have been able to discover it, is not particularly startling, nor do we have 'amazing revelations' to put before you. Nevertheless, one has a duty to be as precise and objective as possible; otherwise, this publication could become a mere eulogy of the town's activities during the war. Such documents are very interesting for the people concerned but are of little wider value.

Modern documentation can create research problems. The main sources, the Civil Defence records, are rather difficult to handle due to their uncatalogued state. Rural District Council records and newspaper accounts, on the other hand, tend to be overwhelming in their complexity and quantity, However, we did have the advantage of dealing with a period which was within living memory and could therefore make use of personal written testimony and tape-recorded interviews. This, in some ways, has double-edged benefits. On the one hand, it adds more immediacy to our study and a stronger sense of human involvement. On the other hand, we run the risk of getting it wrong and being found out—many of the participants are still alive. We take any responsibility for mistakes in fact and are happy to accept correction. Disagreements which local residents might feel about the interpretation of the evidence should be directed towards the editor.

As with all local studies, the material soon became far too much to handle. Limitations were needed. Geographically, we decided to concentrate basically on the town itself and its immediate hinterland. However, the nature of the sources made it quite difficult for us to be consistent in our aim. Until about June 1940 much of the official material concerns Hailsham as the centre of its Rural District. Meetings of the R.D.C's various committees therefore cover an area from Heathfield to Willingdon and from Ninfield to Selmeston. In terms of military defence it was part of the 'C' sub-area which covered an even wider region, namely the coast between Newhaven and Pevensey with the country behind it. Sometimes, newspaper articles contained relevant material from East Sussex in general. Material from these wider regions has been included where it seems relevant. However, from the summer of 1940 onwards, Hailsham comes to be seen as an invasion target. The town becomes a defensive area with its own guarded perimeter. Statistics, thereafter, tend to refer to this much smaller area which actually leaves out parts of the built-up section of the town.

Chronologically, we decided to concentrate on the period between the outbreak of war in September 1939 and the end of

1941. To have continued thereafter would have meant that a great deal of our material would simply have been more of the same sort of thing. Furthermore, by this time, the war had become much more of a global conflict with the participation of the Soviet Union and the United States and from Hailsham's point of view the threat of invasion no longer existed. Events after 1941 are referred to only where they are necessary to follow a particular process to its conclusion or where events are of special interest. I would like to thank the members of the Hailsham History Group who have made this study possible. As a full-time history teacher I have welcomed the forum they have provided for actually doing history rather than just reading about it. They have been patient, painstaking and tolerant under conditions considerably less than ideal.

The members have been as follows:

Mr R.G. Alder	Mrs D. Pope
Mrs M. Alder	Mr J. Pratt
Captain R. Baker	Mr L.R. Smith
Mrs K. Bloomfield	Mrs H. Squier
Mrs M.J. Fanaroff	Mr A. Watson
Mr C.N.F. Gross	Mrs J.V. Watson
Mr E. Pitcher	Mrs D.J. White

We would like to express our particular appreciation of Captain Baker's work. His sad death in 1982 is deeply regretted in the town and he is missed by the Group. His intelligent enthusiasm and skill in seeking out evidence were an example to us all and his charming sketches are distributed throughout this publication.

We also thank the people of the Hailsham area who contributed memories either in writing or on tape. Some were actually members of the group and others now live in the surrounding area. They are:— Mr N. Allen, Mrs A. Mobbs, Captain R. Baker, Mr E. Pitcher, Major O.A. Batten, Mrs B. Rigelsford, Mr A.F. Burgess, Mr J. Roberts, Mr F. Clark, Mrs O. Rous, Mr R. Dodds, Mr S. Salvage, Mr J.D. Faulkner, Mr M.G. Scroggie, Mrs O. Hanks, Dr H.F. Shaw, Miss N. Knowles, Mrs D. Walker, Mr T. Marchant, Mr D. White, Mr W. Marshall, Mrs D. White, Mr H. Maryan, Mr T. Henry Wilson

George Farebrother,

Hailsham School   August 1985

The Hailsham area 1939-40

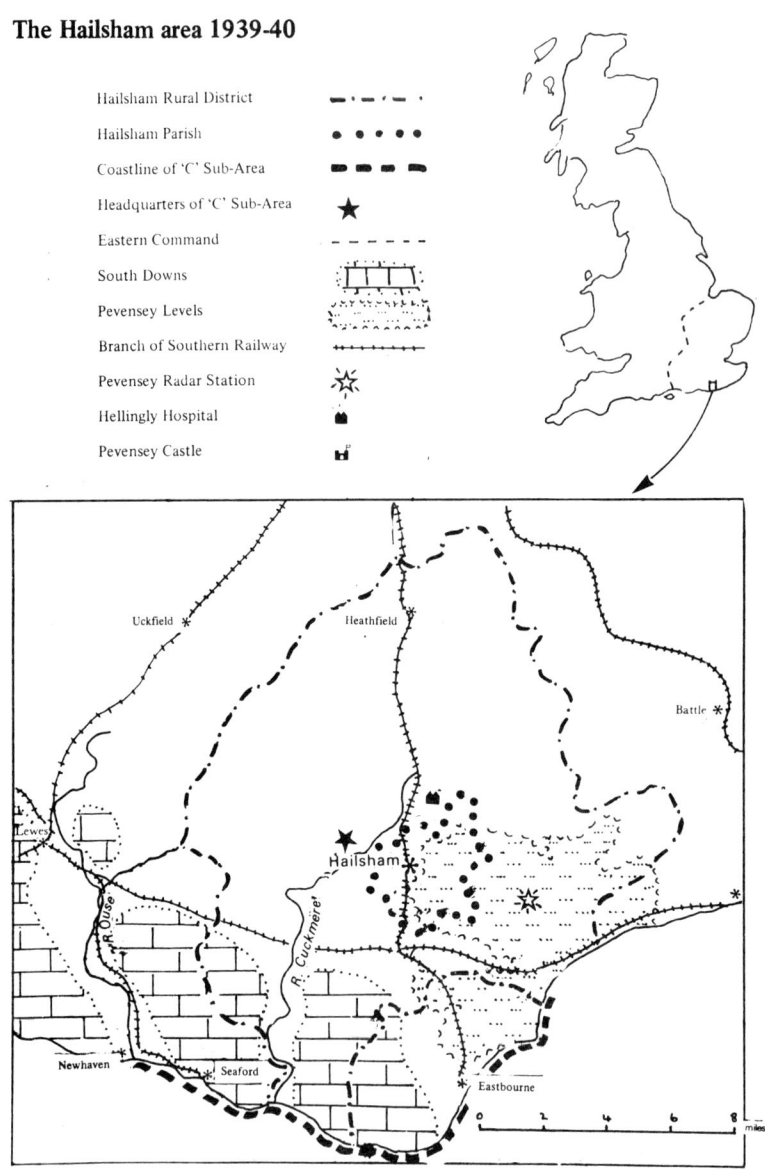

CHAPTER ONE
A Small Market Town

There was a great frost in Sussex from 22nd December 1939 to 4th February 1940, the most severe experienced so far this century. On 29th December an air temperature of 7 degrees F. was recorded and skating began about that time and continued for the next five weeks. Throughout January, 29 ground frosts occurred and the sea was frozen off the coast. Frozen rain fell during the night of 27th-28th of January and blades of grass appeared as glass rods; each twig and branch was totally encased in ice. Telephone wires were each estimated to carry 80-90 pounds of ice between adjacent posts. As a result, wires were down for mile after mile and hundreds of poles were either uprooted or snapped off. Birds were seen frozen by their feet to branches of trees where they had roosted the previous night and they vainly fluttered their wings in their efforts to fly away. Fantail pigeons had to be released from the roof of a house to which they had frozen. Rooks were reported to have fallen from trees with their wings frozen together. Live sheep were seen frozen by their wool to gorse bushes on the Downs.[1]

Such extremes of nature traditionally prefigure cataclysmic events in human affairs. One is reminded of the hairy-tailed comet of 1066, the year in which three kings were alive and two dead in England. With hindsight, we can see these strange phenomena, coming as they did during the uneasy winter of 1939-40, when wartime activity was comparatively muted, as omens of the violence to come. However, it is our business to focus our minds on the town of Hailsham in the dramatic events (or, in some cases, dramatic non-events) which were to follow.

On the eve of the Second World War, Hailsham was a small market town in East Sussex. It was connected by rail to Eastbourne, 8 miles to the south, and to London via Tunbridge Wells. It looked to Lewes, 13 miles to the west, as the county town. Its parish church was modest and much restored by the Victorians but it contained some quite nice stained glass most of which was to be destroyed by bombing in 1943. The town was small but the market itself was significant. It played an important regional, if not national, role. During the 19th century it had been moved from the High Street to a three acre site in Market Street.[2] Cattle and sheep sales were held on alternate Wednesdays and there was also a weekly market for poultry and eggs. This made Hailsham a focus as a shopping area for a region roughly coincident with the Rural District which had its offices at Cortlandt in George Street. This was soon to become the Civil Defence Control Room, much sandbagged, and the officials housed there naturally slid into a wartime role.

The market, drawing on the surrounding agricultural region, was central to the life of the town. It is not surprising, then, that there was a commercial area around the central crossroads where the medieval town must have grown up and another small cluster of such activity at Kirby Croft Chambers in North Street. There were three banks and nine firms of solicitors, as well as a fair share of insurance agents, building societies and estate agents, one of which had for many years acted as the market auctioneer. Hailsham was a seven-pub town and its catering establishments, mainly of the tea and cakes variety, did their busiest trade on market day. More substantial meals were best obtained in 'The George' and 'The Crown'.

One could hardly call Hailsham a centre for manufacturing. Most industrial activity was carried out by the two firms of Green's and Burfield's who made rope, twine, sacking and deck-chairs. The last mentioned resulted in a curious but useful contribution to the war effort, as we shall see later, but there was no danger of Hailsham becoming a prime target for enemy bombers. Other industry was on a very minor level. There were a couple of tile and brick makers - the last of a declining local tradition based on the Wealden Clay - and a few firms making trug-baskets. This was something of a cottage industry. Judging by the inter-war houses in London Road and the fact that there were 20 small firms connected with building, the town seems to have been expanding.

The High Street had much the same appearance then as it does today except that Vicarage Field was an open space and not the site of a shopping precinct. With one or two exceptions, such as the Co-op, there were no national chain stores or supermarkets. Retail outlets tended to be owner-occupied and more numerous then than they are now. For instance, there were seven butchers, eight grocers, and five green-grocers. The town and its outskirts contained no fewer than fourteen small general stores. All this was to create a planning headache under wartime rationing conditions. The town seems to have been surprisingly well off for medical facilities, with four dentists and as many as eight doctors, many of whom were in partnership and doubled as Public Vaccination Officers.

The farming influence was still strong. J.S.O. Robertson-Luxford J.P. Esq. and Lieutenant-Colonel Roland Vaughan Gwynne, D.S.O., D.L., J.P., were prominent landowners, but most of the land in the area was farmed by smaller freeholders and tenant farmers. There were 22 of these in the immediate vicinity. There was quite a strong element of fruit-growing and market-gardening both in the town and just outside. Throughout history, Hailsham has never been a 'closed parish' of the sort dominated by one or two squires. There were, however, prominent figures who were, by their leading position in society, to play a notable part in the war. One of these was the aforementioned Lt. Col. Gwynne, who is still spoken of in hushed tones; he seems to have been quite a fearsome figure. Chairman of the Hailsham Petty Sessions and also of the Rural District Council, his opinions on various aspects of the war effort were to become prominent in local press reports. He was fearless in his condemnation of offenders against blackout regulations but was outspoken in his strictures against official bungling. Another ubiquitous figure was Captain C.F. Gardner, of 'Summertree', Bodle Street, who was a Justice of the Peace and Vice-Chairman of the Hailsham R.D.C. He must have had some military experience as he became prominent in the setting up of the Hailsham Home Guard and was later designated as the military commander, with full powers of martial law should the town ever be invested by enemy troops. The Vicar, the Rev. Macklin Charles Chapman, M.A., of St. Peter's College, Cambridge, lived in the handsome Georgian vicarage, At £542 per annum he was certainly one of the town's wealthier residents. His role made him a crucial factor in civilian wartime activity. The town also had Roman Catholic, Methodist, Baptist and Congregational churches. The Clerk to the R.D.C. was Alfred Carr. During the war years he became the lynchpin of Hailsham's Civil Defence effort and our documentation concerning him is extensive.

The railway station was an important adjunct of the market. The old cattle pens have only in recent years been taken away, but the station itself was closed down during the late 60's. There was a little cluster of pubs and catering establishments around it, and the presence of a railhead accounts for there being seven coal merchants in the town as well as four corn merchants.

There was a small scatter of shops offering various services, probably aimed partly at farmers' wives on market days - ladies' hairdressers, jewellers and a laundry, The limited shopping facilities seem to have been sufficient for the town and its surrounding countryside and people only rarely felt the need to shop in Eastbourne or Brighton. Few people from outside the immediate area seem to have visited the town very much. Hotel accommodation was limited to a couple of pubs and there was only one apartment house. Some tone was added to the town by the existence of a dancing school for girls. There were two tiny private schools, one of which could be traced back to the mid-nineteenth century. In addition, there were three local authority schools: for infants at the corner of North and High Street, for juniors at Grovelands and for seniors at Battle Road. The fate of the scholars at these schools during air raids was to cause much controversy.

The town had its fair share of social organisations. Some, such as the British Legion and the Memorial Institute, were closely connected with the Great War of a generation before. Hailsham boasted a brass band and a 'coffee tavern'. There was a free library, and, strongly associated with it, the Women's Institute, later to become the focus of much war-directed activity.

Such then, was the town which was to be exposed to the stress of war. In the event, anticipation and planning caused far more anxiety than the reality justified. The invasion never came, and bombing raids were very limited. Hailsham tended to be a place where aircraft unloaded their spare bombs on the way back from London. Evacuation from other war-threatened areas in the country caused far more serious difficulties. How the town and its social organisations dealt with the anticipated terrors and the very real problems of war is the subject of this study.

CHAPTER TWO

A Land Sore Troubled

The most ancient legends in the language of the English people speak of a venerable kingdom threatened by a monster from the deep. In the summer of 1940, this monster bore the code name 'Sea Lion'. This *nom de guerre* emphasised the amphibious nature of the proposed German attack on Southern Britain. More than 40 years later we can still study its details with interest. The brigadier in charge of 'C' Sub-Area, which covered the stretch of coast between Newhaven and Pevensey Bay, could only have wished for some fairy godmother to deliver the German plans into his in-tray at headquarters in Upper Dicker.[3]

Field Marshal von Brauschitch was the German officer in charge of Sea Lion and his plans involved an invasion front between Folkestone and Worthing. How would an invasion have affected the 'C' sub-area of which Hailsham was a part? The map which is reproduced below, as well as a study of von Brauschitsch's instruction for the prosecution of Sea Lion, dated 30th August 1940, gives a fair idea of what was to be expected in East Sussex. The tone of this directive is properly magisterial. 'The aim of this attack is to eliminate the Mother Country as a base for continuing the war against Germany and, if it should be necessary, to carry out a complete occupation'. Although it was recognised that negotiated peace was still possible, an attack at any time after 15th September was envisaged. The task was given to Army Group A, already stationed in the Low Countries and north-east France. This comprised the 16th and 9th Armies and between them they were to seize an initial beach head along the central spine of the Weald from Ashford, through Uckfield and into Hampshire. Their first objective after this was to secure the south-east region of England along the line of the North Downs to Portsmouth. London would then be outflanked and the rest of the country subdued thereafter.

From the point of view of East Sussex, the main threat would

The Final Plan for Operation Sea Lion, September 1940

have come from the 9th Army under General Strauss. The first wave of this would consist of four infantry divisions, (including one mountain division), followed up by two panzer and a motorised division. This army would assault the coast between Bexhill and Worthing, but whether it would disembark east or west of Eastbourne was left to the discretion of more junior commanders at the time. Von Brauschitsch's assessment of the situation was suitably crisp: 'After local bridgeheads have been won, energetic junior commanders will co-ordinate the mixed units and will win important features inland. Gradually, weak but coherent groups will form ... heavy counter-attacks by the enemy equipped with artillery are to be expected and heavy weapons will soon come into action'.[4]

It seems clear that the German army over-estimated British powers of resistance at this point. At the end of May 1940, 'C' Sub-Sector was part of a division of Eastern Command. This division comprised much of Sussex, Surrey and Eastern Kent. As most of the Field Army was still in France, the only regular unit in the whole region was 45 Division. This itself had just been moved in from Dartmoor, having recently finished training. A letter from 'C' Sub-Area of 16th July 1940 mentions the 134th Infantry Brigade. There is also reference to a 'mobile reserve'.[5] This, no doubt, refers to the group of units loosely distributed over the central Weald, comprising 1st Army Tank Brigade, 1st Armoured Division (recently moved in from the Portland area), and the 1st Canadian Division which had just moved rather breathlessly from the Aldershot area to the Midlands and then South to the general area area of Horam.[6] 134 Infantry Brigade seems to have overlapped at least some of 'C' Sub-Area command. An undated memorandum by Lt. Col. C.W. Healey, who commanded 190 Field Ambulance refers to it as lying between Pevensey Bay and Bexhill. According to this document, the Brigade seemed to consist of three battalions, namely the 8th Devon, the 6th Devon and the Royal Iniskillin Fusiliers.[7]

The comings and goings of this time are well illustrated through personal memories. Ron Dodds of Eastbourne joined the Royal Sussex Regiment in 1940. First he was stationed at Seaford, but then the unit moved to Yorkshire. Then on the 14th September the regiment was moved to the south coast due, apparently, to an invasion scare. Ron, who was a despatch rider, had his home at

Hankham and was overjoyed to find that his destination was Battle. There was a rest stop at Mayfield where they were given tea and cake by the nuns at the convent. There was also a nice lady in the area who was willing to give hot baths to soldiers in her front room, complete with personalised back-washing. Battle at this time was full of military activity and Ron's unit camped in the grounds of the Abbey. One of his first jobs on arrival was to ride along the convoy counting the vehicles. He found that out of 35 motor bikes only 16 remained, many men having skipped home for the night as their families lived locally. Ron soon found himself posted on the marshes where he had the tedious job of guarding the foreshore. This, however, could be relieved by unofficial visits home.[8]

Mr Pitcher, who worked as a boy in a small shop in Horsebridge, was aware of the influx of troops into East Sussex during September:

> It was not unusual to go to bed at night with a convoy of transports or marching troops going by, wake up in the morning and still find them passing by and quite likely this would continue all day. You would go to work in the morning and find soldiers and guns in the fields which had been empty the day before. I remember going to work on my cycle one such morning, weaving my way between the lorries, guns and bren-gun carriers and passing soldiers having their breakfast by the roadside ... one large patch of grass was packed with sleeping troops. I went into the shop and started my usual morning job of sweeping up when I had that feeling of being watched. On looking up, the whole length of the shop double-front window was lined with white staring faces. These belonged to soldiers who were using the window as a shaving mirror.[9]

The Regular Army units were supplemented by the Home Guard, first referred to as the Local Defence Volunteers, or L.D.V, ('look, duck, vanish', according to some informants). Mr Maryan remembers being sent on an officers' training course at Osterley Park Training School in the summer of 1940. This was a course for future Home Guard Officers.[10] Fortunately, some summary notes of these lectures have survived and they give us some idea of how the Home Guard saw itself. Essentially they were irregulars on the pattern of the American Revolutionary Minutemen or the Peninsular War guerrillas. It was pointed out that the Germans had threatened ruthless reprisals if the Home Guard were to fight them in any way. In fact, they refused to consider the Home Guard as soldiers and there was, it is true, some doubt about their status under the Geneva Convention. The lecturers at Osterley Park were at great pains to point out that members should not be squeamish about such things as killing enemy soldiers whilst they were asleep. It might even be necessary to blow up a vehicle driven for the Germans by one's friend under duress.[11]

The trouble about the Home Guard was that its irregular status was emphasised by its lack of official officers. They could all too easily be regarded as franc tireurs by the enemy and shot out of hand.[12] Actual members were quite capable of regarding their functions in a more satirical light, in Hailsham at least:

> Members of the unpaid, unfed, un-thanked, part-time, part-worn, shirtless army known as the Home Guard are supposed, in the first place, to be crack shots with a rifle, to know the weight, characteristics, contents, parts, and destructive powers of several kinds of bombs. Many are supposed to be expert machine-gunners and are meant to be tommy-gunners. There are many other weapons they are supposed to use and although 1,700,000 men know about them they are far too secret to be mentioned here.[13]

The Home Guard started with a speech by Anthony Eden in May 1940 which asked for volunteers. Mr Maryan says that he joined before the broadcast was actually finished as he lived near the police station, (where the Court House now is). Even then, there was already someone in front of him.[14] Captain Baker had been at sea for several years and found himself at a loose end at this time and rather annoyed that he had not been asked to help at the Dunkirk evacuation and he became one of the first to enlist.[15] Jack Roberts had been unable to get into the army and he too joined up on the day of Eden's broadcast on May 14th. He ended up as acting Quarter Master. Major Batten rather defuses the drama of the situation by pointing out that he too was at the police station immediately Eden's broadcast was over. The police, apparently, knew nothing about it. They were even unwilling to take his name as no forms had arrived yet and asked him to return in a day or two; and so the Major went home. The next morning, Captain Gardner, in charge of the Hailsham Company at the start, asked him to volunteer and the following Sunday there was some sort of turnout at Summertree.[16] Major Batten ended up in charge of No.7 platoon of 'E' Company and his name appears as such on an undated nominal role.[17]

Miss N. Knowles remembers trying to cope with the onrush of volunteers with only a typewriter and a few enrolment forms as equipment.[18] She seems to have done her clerical work at No.1 London Road, an empty house at the time and used as the Home Guard headquarters for a while. It was also conveniently near 'The Grenadier' which continued to act as an unofficial meeting place. Later on, the meetings took place at the newly-completed drill hall in London Road. In charge of the whole 20th Sussex Battalion, which covered an area as large as the Rural District, was Lt. Col. Johnson, D.S.O., who retired in August 1941. His place was taken by Lt. Col. Crompton who had previously been the commander of Headquarters or 'E' Company at Hailsham. However, Captain Gardner continued to be the senior military officer for the town should it actually come under attack by the enemy.[19]

Feelings are mixed about the 'Dad's Army' image of the Home Guard. After all, the men gave up a lot of their time, and all for no pay beyond basic expenses. For more than four years the 20th Battalion stood ready to assemble day or night. Within a short space of time 1,000 fully armed and equipped Home Guards could be mustered within 90 minutes.[20] Jack Roberts remembers being on shift work at Green Brothers with Home Guard training weekends and fire duty on some evenings in front of the Post Office or on top of the Church tower. This left little time for family life.[21]

However, the early days of the Home Guard do give rise to a sense of mild hilarity if we are to go by the stories of surviving participants. They, themselves, readily admit this. On the first parade, members were asked to tie white handkerchiefs around their left arms. Major Batten pointed out that this would be a certain way to be shot. He was told that they would soon be issued with a brassard showing the letters 'L.D.V'. They were then requested to contribute any firearms they happened to possess. Major Batten had a couple of rifles and a shotgun or two. These were immediately shared around the eight members of his own patrol. Cartridges for the shotguns were handed out. These contained twelve balls 'as big as small marbles - guaranteed to stop anyone at twenty yards ... These big balls were likely to take the

L.D.V. assembles before Church Tower Watch

end of the gun off and fire them back in your face. If you didn't kill the man attacking you, you would certainly kill yourself'.[22] Captain Baker seems to have joined a little later. At this stage there were denim overalls and ancient Canadian Ross rifles. The normal British Army calibre bullet did not fit these; 'but this didn't matter as we had none anyway'. Eventually they were issued with five rounds per man. According to Captain Baker, 'we were now set to repel the invasion'.[23] Major Batten had some experience with firearms and was asked to 'zero' them. This proved to be exceptionally difficult as there simply were not enough bullets to test-fire them.[24]

There were two basic night duties. One section kept watch from the top of the church tower. From here there was a fine view over the Pevensey Levels. They looked for anything which might be thought suspicious, especially when aircraft passed over, 'in case anything fell out of the sky from them'. They were also able to use binoculars to spy on courting couples but that was not part of the war effort! This section had a tent in the churchyard among the gravestones. Although it was summertime it could be cold and members of the section padded themselves up so much with sweaters and thermos flasks that it really was impossible for two of them to pass on the tower's spiral staircase. In the state of heightened tension, even the bells and the workings of the Church clock could seem rather eerie in the darkness. The other task was to protect the Post Office from possible acts of sabotage. This was an important duty because the telephone exchange was a vital link in the communications system of the area. Sentries were posted at night outside and no one was supposed to approach it without being challenged. Anyone coming along to post a letter had to hand it to the sentry for inspection to ensure that it contained no explosives.[25]

Of course, there was considerable emphasis on drill. There still seem to be a few copies of the 'Elementary Drill Memory Card' put away in various drawers in Hailsham. This had been produced by H.M.S.O. for 6d. It covered forming up, falling in, and squad drill. 'Drill is the foundation of discipline and esprit de corps', we are assured. Anxious squad commanders duly studied the rather complex little diagrams presented to them.[26] Training courses admitted that equipment was very limited and a great deal of improvisation would have to take place. There seems to have been considerable anxiety about home-made explosives. Trainees were warned that detonators should be treated with special deference. Fulminate of mercury needed careful handling and fitting it into a fuse was an operation in which inattention could be disastrous. Course notes exhibit an anxiety about the value of 'jam tin bombs' which suggests that experiments with Molotov Cocktails were not always entirely successful. The course instructors were at pains to point out that tanks were not so fearsome as people believed. They could easily be stopped by a row of dinner plates across their path, (the drivers believing these to be land mines). They could then be ambushed with Molotov Cocktails or stick grenades. Failing all else, a crowbar thrust into the tracks could quickly immobilise a tank but trainees were warned to let go of the crowbar in time to prevent themselves being cut in half. Dive bombers, too, were less fearsome than they were made to appear. Their speed of descent made the scatter of machine-gun bullets quite wide, and determined rifle fire could, apparently, quite easily scare them off.[27]

Captain Baker's first experience of Molotovs took place on the school field at Battle Road. He didn't feel very convinced that the weapon would be effective as the tank was represented by a couple of sheets of corrugated iron, not very securely fixed, and most of the bottles bounced off without breaking—'but we did a lot of damage to the grass'. The following Sunday parade took place at Woodside where there was a road block. 'We hid among the trees to await the enemy tank. This appeared before long and consisted of a bren-gun carrier manned by the local garrison who had entered into the spirit of the thing and dressed themselves up in a weird assortment of gear intended to be something like panzer uniform'. As soon as they became aware of the ambush they feigned death or terror as their acting abilities permitted.[28] Major Batten remembers a similar occasion at Bodle Street: 'We were set digging trenches beside the road ... The idea was that if a tank came up the road, then you lobbed a Molotov Cocktail at it. We had another group of men in the churchyard. I told them it was the battiest idea I had ever seen. Well, after we had dug these trenches, a fortnight afterwards, we were sent back to fill them in and turf them over again'. The Major seems to have had no inhibitions about making his feelings known because, 'a fresh defensive position was being manned at Prinkles Farm where we were supposed to keep our eye open for tanks coming up the road from Ashburnham way. The first thing we were supposed to do was to send a man up the old oak tree. If he saw a tank he was to run towards us. As I predicted, that idea died the death as well'.[29] A surviving photograph shows Jack Roberts about to load a petrol bomb onto a 'Molotov Slinger'. This machine was invented by Private Green and seems to owe its inspiration to medieval siege engines. It hurled the bomb for some distance but would have been fairly useless, according to Major Batten, owing to the time it took to load up the slinger.

There seems to be general agreement that after the early teething troubles the Home Guard developed into a considerably more respectable organisation. The 20th Battalion duplicated its own news sheet entitled 'BLAST' which was issued twice monthly. A surviving copy from September 1941 seems to have been distributed by Mr Maryan. The wartime paper shortage is emphasised by the requirement that the publication is to be returned to H.Q. within a fortnight. This news sheet notes the improvement in rifle shooting and describes a competition between the various companies. The Hailsham Company, regrettably, came last although one of its members, Sergeant Gibbs, obtained the highest score. Members were told how to oppose enemy air landings and warned about the

German gambit of dropping 'incendiary leaves'. These were wafers of celluloid and smoked rubber, covered with phosphorus, which ignited when the dew had evaporated from them in the morning. A new weapon, the 'Smith Gun', was also described. It was very mobile and could fire a 7lb. anti-personnel bomb.[30] The third anniversary celebration of the formation of the Home Guard saw a demonstration of spigot mortars, described as a 'powerful anti-tank weapon'. The Home Guard was clearly past the broomstick and pike stage by this time.[31] Tommy-guns, especially useful in street fighting, were in wide circulation by 1941. Major Batten recalls that if you pulled the trigger halfway down they would lock and continue firing. Apparently the first man in his section to use it locked the mechanism by mistake and turned round with it still firing to ask what to do. He would have shot the whole platoon had somebody not pushed the gun down.[32]

One mystery which is very difficult to penetrate is that of the 'Special Groups'. These were under the control of Section D, a secret department of the Foreign Office. Its purpose was 'to investigate the possibilities of subversion and sabotage in enemy-held territory'. After the fall of France, thoughts of turning these techniques to Britain itself began to emerge. A complete secret army, ready to harass any part of Britain which became occupied by the Germans, was set up. Regional Commissioners, who had been appointed by the Government to run the country in the event of general collapse, were in the know, as well as Chief Constables and senior local officials. Cells, known as 'Auxiliary Units', and consisting of five or six men, were formed. Although they were given official Home Guard designation, they were really quite separate from that organisation, merely using it as a cover. These units would literally go underground to prepared positions which were rather like modern nuclear shelters complete with weapons, food and every other means of survival. Local people, with intensive knowledge of the countryside—poachers as well as gamekeepers—were trained in techniques of sabotage.[33] There was certainly considerable emphasis on guerilla warfare in the lectures given at Osterley Park in 1940. 'Invisible destruction' was emphasised:

> Remember that the guerilla has to work like a ghost. He has to undermine the morale of the enemy by being always unexpected and dangerous. If the Nazis seize an English

county, we must make it impossible for them to send despatches about that county without an escort of armoured cars.[34]

It must have been this very course which Mr Maryan remembers attending in August 1940. He was still in possession of the notes in 1980 and recalls being made an Intelligence Officer on his return from the course. He knew about the Special Groups at the time. One of them was reported by a rather puzzled Home Guard at Lower Dicker, This man had discovered a large dugout and didn't quite know what to do about it. The incident had to be hushed up rather firmly.[35] Major Batten was certainly not aware of what was going on, but he guessed that 'something was afoot' when some of his best N.C.O's were taken off for 'special training' and never seen on regular Home Guard duty again. In the 1960s he was on the County Defence Committee which briefly considered the aforementioned dugouts at Park Wood as a Centre of Regional Government in the event of nuclear attack. Mr Roberts refers to the features in Park Wood as an 'underground city' and believes that it was originally built by the Canadians stationed at Horam. It is not clear, however, how much of this knowledge came to him at the time, and how much leaked out after the war.[36] It is certainly very difficult to find evidence in Park Wood today.

A wartime landlord of a pub on the edge of the marshes was interviewed about his activities by a member of our group. The whole interview is worth recording in full, with only slight editorial alteration:

> I was approached by the head of this local organisation and asked if I would co-operate with them. That's how it really started. It's very difficult—I'd rather not mention any names. I don't know whether I should. It was an Eastbourne person who approached me and they'd got a wireless station in the place where he worked upstairs, and he sent out information. Another place we went to was a big farm with a wireless set upstairs and they would have been able to transmit information. We also went to this farmhouse several times for lectures. The Army came and gave us these lectures about what we were to expect and what we were to do ... When we had these meetings, there were twenty or thirty of us all turned up, but I didn't know where they came from. They must have been dotted about all over the area. I had contacts

with someone in Bodle Street and the head one at Eastbourne. There were also contacts at Stone Cross and Normans Bay.

The idea was that we'd carry on with our work as if nothing was happening and then if there was any information we could go to our next contact and inform them. The one with the wireless station was in the Stone Cross area, (there was also a contact in Bodle Street). A good excuse to get to Bodle Street was to take the horse to the blacksmith, and then they wouldn't suspect anything. We had secret places where we could leave a message ... and this reduced the risk of exposure. The fellow from down the coast could quite easily come in and have a pint of beer and give me the wink and the message could be left somewhere else. He was a 'looker' on the coast.

All these people that I knew then are now dead. I don't want to divulge their names. There was just a single person in each place, not a group. We had no secret hiding place. Their idea was that we would carry on working as normal. That's what the Army told us, that the Germans would expect us to go on working ... Being a publican I had the local Home Guard always trying to get me in the Home Guard and they put forward my name as a recruit: but I was sworn to secrecy and couldn't tell them what I was doing. They put my name in several times and it was always turned down ... I got rather unpopular with some of the Home Guard chaps. One chap, a farm worker, was going to give me a hand with some corn carrying, and when I asked him he said, 'no, I wouldn't care to come and give *you* a hand', That was because I wasn't in the Home Guard. But you had to be so secretive about it. That was one of the most important things they stressed. If anything had leaked out they'd shoot you, wouldn't they?[37]

All of this suggests that there was not only a group of men ready to take military action in the event of occupation but also a complete information network ready, presumably, to maintain contact with the hopefully undefeated British mobile reserve. This network shows the classical characteristics of a resistance group organised in cells for security and probably owes something to experience gained in the Spanish Civil War. The emphasis on

The Home Guard Change of Watch on Church Tower

keeping out of the Home Guard was probably due to the fact that members would have automatically been under suspicion from the German occupiers and might have been shot as saboteurs anyway.

Meanwhile, the dangerous summer of 1940 saw the Commander of 'C' Sub-Area attempting to manipulate his woefully inadequate resources. A secret circular of July 16th addressed to all his subordinate commanders starts off confidently enough:

> The general policy is to destroy the enemy on the beach and to stop his airborne invasion from attacking the beach defences in the rear.

The general policy behind local thinking seems to owe more to the philosophy of Alan Brooke than to the planning of General Ironside who was still officially in command of Home Defence and would not be replaced until July 18th. For instance, there is mention of a 'mobile reserve' in the course of formation and training. There is considerable emphasis on the construction of 'fortresses', the precursors of the 'Nodal Points' discussed in the next chapter. The object of these fortresses, defended by dragons' teeth, was to force enemy armour into exposed positions. There was clearly a shortage of these concrete anti-tank pyramids at the time:

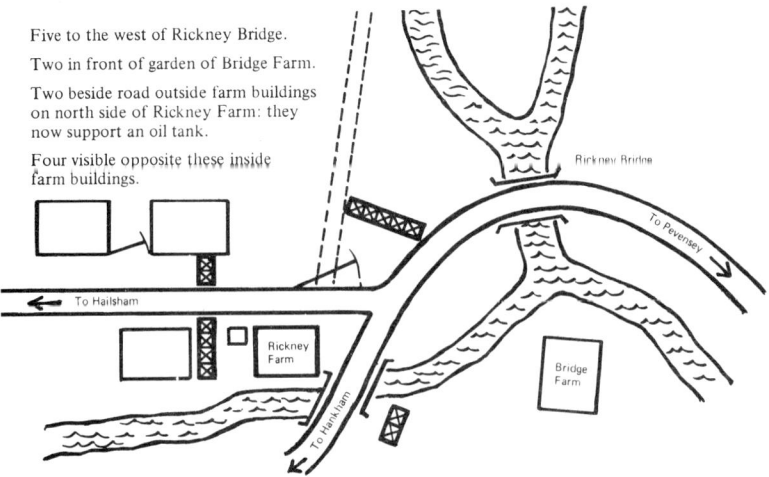

Anti-tank Barrier Remaining at Ricknay, November 1979.
'Sharks' or 'Dragons' Teeth

production would have to be speeded up. The Hailsham by-pass had been constructed but was not yet open. By using dragons' teeth it was intended to deny its use to the enemy. Pevensey Castle was to be made '100 per cent tank-proof' and it was hoped that the enemy would be unable to approach within 2,000 yards of it. This venerable ruin had a part in previous invasions of Britain from late Roman times onwards. It featured in the events of 1066: and in 1940 the Roman ruins were disguised as machine-gun posts. A careful inspection today can still reveal several cunningly concealed slits facing in the general direction of abroad. The Area Commander emphasised the need for booby traps, especially at Birling Gap. The shortage of weapons at this period is underlined by the need for shingle projectors, weapons for hurling the beach at the enemy. More barbed wire was needed to keep men with grenades out of firing range and minefields were to be guarded, but not labelled as dangerous to the public. Such notices would have been far too useful to the Germans. However, some places *not* mined were to be labelled in order to confuse agents. Attention was drawn to the danger of espionage and the Irish in particular were suspected of being secretly in sympathy with the Germans. It was made quite

Gun positions at Pevensey Castle

clear that the public were to be discouraged from photographing or 'gazing at' defensive positions.[38]

Another circular sent out on 22nd July again strikes an optimistic note: 'our object is to surprise and destroy the invaders absolutely': no nonsense there. This time, great emphasis was placed on the need for deceit. Real defences were to be concealed, especially from air observation, and dummy defences, 'suitably manned with dummies', were to be left where they could be seen. It was emphasised that these dummies should be shifted about and their positions altered in order to prevent precise duplication on successive air photographs. Home Guards, at this time, must have been kept busy stuffing straw into old uniforms and moving them about the countryside. In a similar way, they were encouraged to paint false gunslits onto unoccupied house fronts; one imagines that the owners of nearby occupied houses would have complained about this. Many types of artillery and anti-aircraft guns had been placed on top of Martello towers on Pevensey Bay and these too had to be disguised. Clearly, these old Napoleonic defences were capable of serving another turn. Mention is made of the pill boxes on the Pevensey Levels and many of these still survive, especially in the Rickney area.[39]

A significant military centre in the Sub-Area was, surprisingly, Hellingly Hospital. It was, in fact, the headquarters of a succession of Royal Army Medical Corps units. By the day war broke out the 21st General Hospital Unit was organised under Mr T. Henry Wilson, O.B.E.,T.D.,M.B.,B.S.,F.R.C.S.,M.R.C.P. He had supervised the appointment of the personnel during the period leading up to the war which consisted at first of people interested in medicine. They were later augmented by pacifists. At first, conditions at Hellingly were primitive. Donald White, a member of the Territorial Army unit at Park House, remembers that:

> At the beginning we had no greatcoats, but we were allowed to use our civilian raincoats and were paid. I think, 1/3d a week for doing so. We slept on bare boards to start with ... As the hospital became operational, bell tents, erected on a strip of land at the perimeter of the garden, were used as sleeping accommodation for the staff ... The house at Union Corner known as 'The Spinney', was taken over, as well at the 'Station Inn', (now 'Golden Martlet').

The winter months of 1939-40 were bitterly cold and there was a severe outbreak of influenza. In February, the unit went to France in the teeth of an outbreak of measles. This was still the period of the 'phoney war' and the unit found itself 15 miles south of Boulogne with little to do but wait for something to happen. It was so cold that they had to dress to go to bed. During late May the German advance threatened to cut them off. Mr Wilson stayed behind to burn papers and to attend to severely wounded troops who were then patched up and sent to the waiting boats at Dunkirk. He was captured and spent the rest of the war in various prisoner-of-war camps. The remnants of the unit straggled back to help out in the hospital and eventually went out to India in 1941 when Park House was handed over to Canadian forces.[40] The nurses at Hellingly were, it seems, the occasion of a fair amount of interest to the various military units in the area.[41]

In spite of the frantic preparations by the Home Guard and Field Army, German soldiers failed to make an appearance on the British mainland. However, there was plenty of air action in the area of the Hailsham Rural District during the Battle of Britain period. The record of deaths due to war operations includes both military and civilian fatalities. The first German airman to die was a 25 year old flier whose parachute failed to open on 29th August. His body was discovered at New Lodge Farm by the 8th Devons. The latter part of September seems to have been a particularly busy period for aerial activity when five German and at least three British airmen were killed in the Hailsham area.[42] The air battles were witnessed by civilians such as Mr Pitcher who, as a boy, stood outside the shop where he worked at Horsebridge watching the formations heading towards London. He recalls that it got very noisy with the whine of diving aircraft and the rattle of machine-gun and cannon fire. A Hailsham housewife remembers with some irritation the anti-aircraft gun stationed on the Gordon Road side of the railway; they were never warned when it was going to fire so that one could leave doors and windows open to prevent flying glass. She was afraid that it would upset her baby daughter and she would therefore take her for long walks on the marshes.[43]

Some of the individual actions are worth mentioning. On September 27th Pilot Officer Neaker, D.F.C., flying out of Chichester, was caught by enemy fire. His parachute failed to open and he fell to his death in Brightling Park. One incident over Hailsham itself has been recalled by several witnesses. It involved Pilot Officer Francis Burton from South Africa. He was chasing a Messerschmidt 110 when he ran out of ammunition. The only way left was to ram the German aircraft; he dived on the enemy, slicing off one of the fighter-bomber's twin tailfins. It crashed into a field near the Station Road sewage works, killing the two crew. Burton was unable to recover from the collision and his aircraft crashed into a massive oak tree at New Barn Farm, Station Road and burst into flames. He received no recognition as the incident was not seen by other military personnel.[44] Several German airmen were buried in Hailsham cemetery but their bodies were reclaimed by their families after the war was over.[45]

Civilians were in some danger from aircraft. Three boys, one of whom was Mr Pitcher, decided to cycle out to see a Me. 109 fighter which had been brought down near Berwick railway station. As they were deciding whether to cross the electric line to get a closer look, the soldier who was guarding it shouted a warning to take cover. At the same time they heard the sound of a plane and, on looking round, saw something fall from it about half a mile away and a large column of smoke coming up. By this time the boys were hiding in the ditch beside the line and the German bomber was flying very low towards them. It opened fire on the crashed plane and the soldier on the ground fired back with his bren-gun. There were flashes as bullets struck the ballast and the metal line, and they saw the face of the German rear-gunner as he peered out firing his machine-guns. Apparently, the real target was the disused Wilmington airfield which at this time was covered with old cars and wagons to prevent it being used for landing enemy troops. Although he did not go back for a return visit Mr Pitcher was excited by seeing a German aircraft so close.[46] Like other boys, he enjoyed the trade in bits of shrapnel and crashed aircraft. However, this sort of thing could go too far and the public were warned against it. Not only could it be dangerous—crashed planes might suddenly blow up—but collectors were actually breaking the law, especially when they started ripping out dials from instrument panels on enemy planes. These could have been of considerable interest to government scientists and as downed German aircraft were Government property these collectors could be prosecuted for theft.[47]

Meanwhile, Hailsham was making its own unique contribution to the war effort. There was a need for dummy aircraft to be spread around airfields to encourage the Germans to waste time bombing them. They had to be capable of fast repair and must cost very little. The design team included technicians from the film industry who were capable of all sorts of deception and the factory chosen was Green Brothers of Hailsham, due to their expertise in making deck chairs - it was the same principle; canvas stretched over folded and hinged wood. Experiments showed that the dummies could be mounted on trestles and still escape detection. Most of the 'aircraft' made were Hurricanes. They were mounted on a light metal stand with wheels so that they could easily be pushed into position. They could be folded up and stacked in the back of a small lorry. Altogether Green Bros. made about 500 of these dummies. They served their purpose well because the company was kept busy making replacements and patching up bullet holes.[48]

If you take the marsh road between Wartling and Pevensey, and turn south near a small farmhouse, you are confronted with a rather bleak landscape dotted with curiously-shaped concrete structures. It is almost as if someone had planned a large-scale exercise in geometrical perspective. There are little groups of truncated pyramids, stark cubes and low lozenge-shaped features.

There are larger earthworks also which can, with some little danger, be penetrated. Inside are twisted steel girders and evidence of electric cables and ventilation shafts. Some areas have been used by the farmer for cattle fodder. It needs some imagination to reconstruct in one's mind the tall pylons and protected buildings which comprised by far the most important strategic structure in the Hailsham area, namely the Radar Station which was one of the chain on the south-east coast which played a vital role in the Battle of Britain.

The correct interpretation of this area requires some understanding of how radar worked. In 1940 the process was called 'Radio Direction Finding'. The local population was quite content with stories of 'death rays', but AMES, or Air Ministry Experimental Stations, were actually intended to measure the time taken for a radio wave to travel from a transmitter aircraft and back again to a receiver. Pevensey was only one of a whole series of stations located near the coast. The R.D.F. operators passed on the heights and positions of enemy aircraft to a central unit at Stanmore. This information then went to Number 11 Group Headquarters at Uxbridge which would then decide on the appropriate response. It is quite clear that the whole structure was essential to the success or failure of the Battle of Britain.

Bearing all this in mind, we can recognise the line of concrete pyramids at the Pevensey end of the area as transmission aerials. These were 360 high and very shaky to climb. One brave individual did succeed in scaling this height in the winter of 1939 to free the structure from ice. The largest concrete block still retains its blast walls. This was the Transmission Block. A similar structure at Rye sustained and survived a direct hit on the top. The rather smaller buildings were receiving blocks and the slightly raised positions on the perimeter supported anti-aircraft guns. The oblong structures, reminiscent of ancient burial mounds, were air raid shelters. People were not eager to use them as they easily flooded to a depth of two or three feet. The whole area was guarded by servicemen and the isolation of the marshes, with only the bleating of sheep for company, was too much for at least one of them who put an end to his life with a service revolver.

The operatives themselves were women. They were recruited with great care because the work required considerable concentration. For instance, the ability to calculate vectors was essential. At first

Surviving Earthworks from the Pevensey Radar Station

they were worked in 12 hour shifts but once real action started in the middle of 1940, these were reduced to 8 hours. The echo appeared as a blip in the straight line shown on a cathode ray tube. There was continuous strain on the eyes. At first many of the women enjoyed themselves but tedium and cold soon set in. However, for most of them, the sense of being chosen for a special task maintained their spirits. There were times of high excitement as well. With experience they could learn to trace the build-up of huge German formations over the English Channel and Northern France. They took hours to coalesce but were broken up in seconds by the defending fighters.

On August 12th 1940 six heavy explosive bombs and three incendiaries dropped on the Pevensey Station. The women themselves were quite aware of what was happening because it was they themselves who plotted the approach of the fighter-bombers. There were casualties and three of the wooden sheds were destroyed, with men buried inside. The operators felt a certain irony when they were informed of the incident by Stanmore - as if they didn't know. The Officer in charge, Flight-Lieutenant Scroggie, was lucky to escape with his life. It was one of the few days when he happened to be away on official duties. His usual car-parking position was bombed and one missile partly penetrated a protected building and his office filled up to a level of ten feet with gravel.[49]

The Civil Defence reports for August 12th state that it was 'difficult to get accurate accounts due to the military taking charge'. Two days later, two ambulances and two First Aid Parties were called to the same station and refused admittance. Secrecy came above all. There was no official acknowledgement of the existence of Radar before 1941 and the Sussex Express commends the ability of the W.A.A.F. radio operators at Pevensey for their discretion about what went on there.[50] It is interesting that two recollections of people connected with Civil Defence contradict the official account by claiming that there were no casualties at the time. The R.A.F. took over the incident immediately and must have made a very good job of keeping the civilians at arm's length. The area around the Radar Station continued to receive more than its fair share of attention. On August 29th an enemy fighter was shot down there and there was a British air crash on September 9th. On September 15th no fewer than 7 bombs were dropped at some unspecified place 'on the marshes' and there were 11 more incidents in the Horseye-Rickney area before the end of November, usually involving large numbers of bombs.[51]

This chapter has, of necessity, concentrated on the wider context of invasion preparations in East Sussex as a whole and especially on the country stretching back from the coastline between Newhaven and Pevensey. The next chapter will consider Hailsham itself in more detail.

CHAPTER THREE

If they should come

Anyone wishing to know how well Hailsham was prepared to meet the German invader during the second year of the war could have spoken to no better person than Alfred Carr, Clerk to the Hailsham Rural District Council: not that the security-conscious Mr Carr would have told you much—his correspondence tended to be marked 'SECRET', not to say 'URGENT'. His letters to the East Sussex County Council, usually addressed to H.S. Martin, the County Civil Defence Controller, or to the South East Regional Commissioner's Office at Tunbridge Wells, betray a conscientious anxiety about the all too easily imagined future. Locked in his office was the sealed envelope containing his instructions in the event of invasion. These were not to be opened until the military order 'Action Stations!' had been given.[1] In the second January of the war, Mr Martin was a very worried man.

As far as he was concerned, the problem was not really a military one. Major C.F. Gardner would have told you more about that side of it. In August 1939, the Major, who was then a Captain, was sitting on the A.R.P. Committees.[2] He was the Chairman of the Hailsham Rural District Council and was instrumental in setting up the Hailsham Home Guard after Dunkirk. He was also a member of the vitally important Civil Defence Emergency Committee.[3] He was the town's Military Commander and he, it seems, who would be responsible for implementing the crucial 'Action Stations' order.[4]

If it was not a military problem, then neither was it a Civil Defence problem. Of course, there was never enough in the way of equipment, and costs were supposed to be minimal but the citizens of Hailsham had rallied round. In January 1941 there were 24 A.R.P. wardens, 2 First Aid parties, a Rescue Party, a Casualty Reception Centre and volunteers trained in gas decontamination. There was still a shortage of stretchers and blankets and 3 portable urinals might be much in demand among a population of 4,500 under fire.[5]

And so the problem was not essentially one of defence. That could be handled, given time and luck. The problem was really political. Mr Carr was still confused about his role during an invasion. This was because Hailsham, in common with other East Sussex towns, was expected to fight. It had been singled out as a 'NODAL POINT'. This was a new, rather bureaucratic sounding phrase. Although these two words occasionally made their appearance before 1941, the usual expression was more often 'fortress',[6] or 'do or die' area.[7] The final definition was arrived at in June 1941, but it is clear that the idea had already existed for at least a year before that. A Nodal point was officially defined as:

> A defended locality, situated usually at strategically important road junctions, garrisoned normally by local Home Guards, with the addition of any available troops stationed in the vicinity, and intended to restrict, delay or hamper the operation of enemy invaders until reserves and reinforcements could be brought up.[8]

A Nodal point was supposed to be self-sufficient for a week because it would be cut off from all outside help.[9] There was definitely a feeling among some of the Home Guard that they were to be something of a sacrifice. The Germans were to be positively encouraged to attack Hailsham. This would keep the enemy busy until the 'real army' turned up.[10] Be that as it may, plans had to be made to care for the civilian population under siege conditions. All of this rather awesome task belonged to Mr Carr. To him, the serious problem was one of responsibility. Some of the basic points had, it was true, been established. Suppose, for instance, that central government were to break down. In this case, normal civil administration would be carried out by the South Eastern Regional Commissioner at Tunbridge Wells. Also, it was quite clear that the Military, Major Gardner in the case of Hailsham, would take over inside the Nodal Point. Under government regulations he had the authority to assume startlingly dictatorial powers. For instance, people could be suddenly moved from one place to another or, alternatively, told to stay put.[11] They could be conscripted to clear debris or shift casualties about.[12] The good people of Hailsham might suddenly find their houses commandeered at a moment's

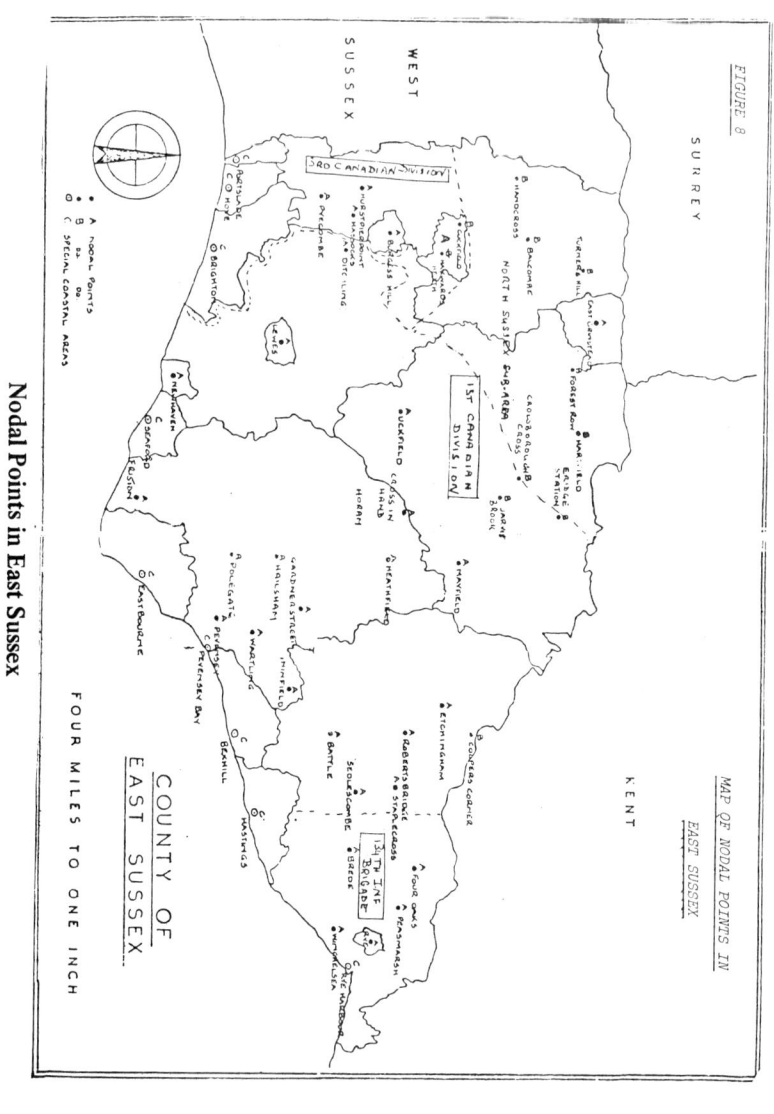

Nodal Points in East Sussex

notice or their lorries used for moving essential supplies. Shopkeepers might easily find some of their foodstocks seized, (albeit, hopefully, in exchange for a receipt). Farmers were not supposed to use their cattle and crops for food 'except in dire emergency', but these could be seized (to prevent their falling into the hands of the enemy'.[13] Citizens jamming their belongings into the car and driving away as quickly as possible from the shelling would have their access to most metalled roads blocked and their attention directed to a field path. This would soon lead them to struggle out of the car. Their last sight of it might be a column of smoke—the police were empowered to destroy vehicles by burning; otherwise they could be useful to the Germans, who were not as motorised as we tend to imagine.[14] The population was certainly expected to cooperate, but obedience would be enforced if necessary.[15]

It was quite clear, then, that conditions under siege would be very different from those of normal bombing. The regular Civil Defence would certainly be unable to cope. Furthermore, the Military Commander would have his hands full with the actual battle itself.[16] It was this situation which led Mr Carr to put his thoughts on paper in January 1941 when writing to the County Controller at Lewes. He had obviously been talking to his counterparts in other towns. There was considerable confusion, it seems, about the position of civilians should there be an attack. 'It seems to me', he pointed out, 'remembering that civilians will still be in residence, in addition to the fighting forces, that provision should be made in each area for water supply, fire fighting, casualties, rescue, decontamination, public health (including sanitation), feeding, shelter. curfew etc...' He went on to emphasise that the boundaries of the area had really been to suit the military—civilian needs were secondary. Everyone, it seems, had agreed that 'something should be done'. Promises had been made and 'points would be taken up'. However, no actual progress had been made. Who, he wondered, would transmit military orders to the civil population? It was the civil authorities, and especially the police, who would have to make sure that things happened as the military ordered; the troops would be too busy fighting Germans: and yet no real machinery had been set up to meet this situation. To make matters worse, there was the problem of security. Now, it is generally agreed that German espionage in Britain was a ludicrous failure. Furthermore, the expected fascist sympathisers failed to materialise. Anyway, those even remotely liable to help the enemy had been interned. However, people's minds at that time were full of images of the Spanish Civil War and the German takeover of Austria. The 'Fifth Column' was very real in their minds. Local military commanders had stressed the need for secrecy in defence preparations—pro-German Irish were their main worry.[17] Propaganda films emphasised the danger of enemy agents disguised as British officers speaking English which was just a little too perfect.

A letter from Tunbridge Wells in May 1940 to Local Authorities had stressed the peril of Germans dropping from the sky disguised as clergymen or women.[18] This, apparently, had happened in the Netherlands. Given this frame of mind, it is not surprising that Mr Carr was determined to accept no orders from a 'stranger in uniform' unless he could produce the proper papers.

Mr Carr had discussed these matters with the R.D.C. Emergency Committee. The main members of this body were Keith Martin, Major (or Captain) Gardner and Lieutenant-Colonel Johnson.[19] The last two were heavily involved in Home Guard duties. They all seemed to agree that a state of chaos would follow an invasion warning. The result of all these worries was the letter written by Mr Carr to County Hall on January 14th 1941. What is significant is that he requested the letter to be forwarded to the War Office.[20] The Emergency Committee itself seems to have been in an awkward position. For the previous two years, under various names such as 'A.R.P.' Committee and then 'Civil Defence Committee', it had happily been setting up First Aid Parties and liaising with the W.V.S. or Fire Brigade; but much of this activity seems to have been directed towards the sporadic damage likely to have been caused by air raids on Hailsham. Would the Committee be called upon to deal with the far more alarming problems of artillery bombardment? No one seemed to know.[21]

All this confusion would have been understandable six months previously. After all, Von Runstedt's Army Group A had been poised on the Pas de Calais ready to strike, apparently, at Hailsham and the rest of South-East England. But the Battle of Britain had been fought and the Germans were beginning to direct their attention towards Operation Barbarossa—the attack on the Soviet Union. It is natural to wonder how an actual invasion in the summer of 1940 would have been dealt with as far as civil administration was concerned; as we have seen, the evidence from 6

The Old Vicarage, Market Street. Sharks Teeth in Front Garden. 1940

months later does not entirely inspire confidence. A memorandum dating from as early as May 1940 makes it clear that the police had extensive powers of directing civilians. Implicit in this memorandum is the assumption of military control in the event of invasion: but nowhere are the precise relationships between local government, the police and the army spelt out. However, perhaps it is all too easy to be unhistorical by viewing the situation from the standpoint of 40 years later. People in early 1941 were still convinced that a German invasion was imminent, once the weather had cleared in the Channel.

They were not to know that Hitler had given up the idea. However, they had been given several months in which to reflect on the more serious implications of military control.

The selection of Hailsham as a Nodal Point cannot be documented before February 1941. However, its origin goes back to the summer of 1940. The Brigadier in charge of 'C' Sub-Area—the military defence region covering the coastline of Eastbourne, Seaford and Newhaven with their hinterland describes Pevensey, Stone Cross, Polegate and Hailsham as 'fortresses'.[22] 'Dragons' teeth', (anti-tank blocks made of concrete), were to be set up in these places. In one paragraph of this letter the words 'Nodal Point' are used for the first time, but only in a generalised way. Hailsham itself is not singled out. At this stage, the Polegate by-pass had not yet been finished. It is suggested that it might be blocked, 'so as to compel the enemy to force his way through a "fortress"'. Hailsham is obviously intended here. This document clarifies the role of Nodal Points and confirms the impression of some Home Guard members that they were meant to be expendable.[23] They were obviously intended to positively attract the attention of the enemy—at considerable cost to themselves.

The actual inner perimeter of Hailsham had already been established by the summer of 1940. It can be traced from the memories of residents and checked from a sketch plan found in the Police headquarters in Lewes. Lying, as it did on the north-west rim of the flat Pevensey Levels, Hailsham occupied an important strategic position, for Pevensey Bay was an attractive location for a seaborne landing and several of the roads across the marsh converge on the town from whence other roads radiate in all directions. Obviously, firm defence of Hailsham was to be expected. It was the first town of any importance able to seriously hamper the enemy's efforts to break out of his bridgehead.

The sketch map (Figure 10) shows that an inner perimeter was established round the town in order to cover all the routes by which traffic could enter or leave. The line was largely formed from dragons' teeth', (sometimes known as 'sharks' teeth'). These were about four feet square and perhaps four and a half feet tall and they were spaced so that there was no room for any vehicle larger than a bicycle to get through. The line of sharks' teeth was not continuous but filled in any gaps between houses, incorporating them to form a continuous line. In 1940 there were many more gaps than there are today and there was a whole section occupied by allotments which needed to be filled in. People found these blocks in their gardens something of an inconvenience, especially if they wanted to go out on a dark night in the blackout to get a scuttle of coal.

Where the lines crossed the roads there were means by which the roads could be half blocked by large concrete structures, the other half being provided with sockets into which heavy steel girders made of railway iron could be fitted to complete the block in case of need.[24]

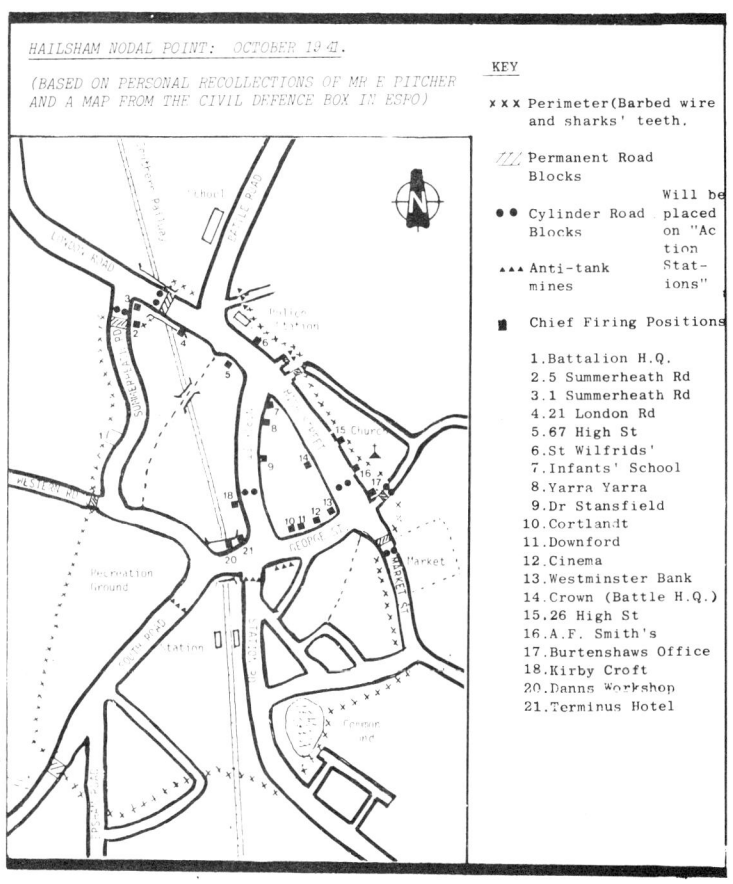

The Hailsham Nodal Point. October 1941

Mr Carr was well aware that this perimeter might answer military needs but it hardly took the needs of the civilian population into account. Miss Rous, who lived at 19, Ersham Road during 1940, was just outside the perimeter. The shark's teeth crossed her road halfway up, just before Knight's Nurseries, along Nursery Path. In the event of invasion, she and her family were supposed to move inside the perimeter, 'if we wished to save our lives'. Only people living inside the perimeter seemed to qualify for free Anderson Shelters.[25] The Casualty Reception Centre in Dr Shaw's house, St Wilfrid's, was just on the perimeter itself. In 1941, the only trained nurse, Mrs Shaw, lived there and most of the 16 auxiliaries would have had to travel inside the Nodal Point. This would certainly have caused confusion in an emergency. It was eventually decided to provide Casualty Reception more centrally in the basement of Kirby Croft Chambers.[26] However, the auxiliaries would still have had to submit to barrier checks. In February 1941 the population inside the Nodal Point was 2,500 and that outside, but still in Hailsham, numbered 2,000. It seems as if enough shelter accommodation for those outside the perimeter had been provided—but only inside the perimeter. One wonders if this would really have been the safest plan.[27] As late as August 1941, strutted basements were still being kept in reserve for 'unexpected influx'. Did this refer to the panic-stricken population outside the perimeter—or to refugees further afield?[28] However, it was not until April 1942 that plans were made to enlarge the perimeter. A Civil Defence report of that date points out that the population still inside the perimeter be increased to approximately 4,000, including garrison.[29]

During the months after Mr Carr's rather dismal letter of January 1941 several problems were taken up. Matters became much clearer. By June of that year the 'Triumvirate' had made its appearance. This consisted of Mr Carr, Inspector J. Morris of the Police and the Garrison Commander, Major Gardner. This body provided the required integration between the various authorities.[30]

The tasks of the triumvirate are carefully laid out in the 'Yellow Book', issued by the South Eastern Regional Office in June 1941. In paragraph 17 the formation of Triumvirates is recommended in Nodal Points. The three members should 'provide together for the safety and welfare of the civil population. To this end they should discuss their problems and make their plans together, the food organiser, the fire chief, the medical man responsible for casualties, and the heads of the A.R.P. services being brought into the picture when their respective responsibilities are under consideration'. The booklet also emphasises that the civil authorities would carry on in the normal way under invasion conditions until 'fighting begins or is imminent'. In Paragraph 20 code words were recommended. 'Stand To' shows the stage at which preliminary preparations should be taking place—evacuation of buildings required by the military, perhaps, or bringing extra civil defence units into a state of readiness. 'Action Stations' was to represent a full alert against the immediate threat of enemy action. These Code words were to be issued by the Regional Commissioner himself. The problem of 'strangers in uniform' was dealt with by making sure that only messages received through the 'usual channels' would be acted on. This was all very well, but Tunbridge Wells could not really give any answer to the question of what would happen if normal communications were to break down. They could only say that, 'Discretion would have to be used locally': officials had been prepared to do this anyway.[31]

The problems, then, were being sorted out; the anxieties of January were being dissolved. The moving spirit behind this co-ordination seems to have been Mr L.D. Burrows who worked from Tunbridge Wells. He travelled the area extensively. Early on in 1941 we find him in Gardner Street, an area which fell under Hailsham's jurisdiction as far as defence was concerned. People like Mr Carr were at this meeting as well as Lieutenant-Colonel Johnson in charge of the 20th battalion of the Home Guard, Mr Ricardo the Chief Warden and Major Alexander, the A.R.P. organiser. Mr Burrows explained the thinking behind Nodal Points and outlined the official 'Stay Put' policy regarding civilians. A careful survey was made of facilities for supplying water, fire fighting, food distribution, Civil Defence services, shelter and dealing with casualties. Although Gardner Street was itself a Nodal Point, it seemed to have no shelter facilities, although there was some talk about slit trenches. Furthermore, no arrangements had been made for gas decontamination and there was not even a First Aid Point.[32]

How far were civilians taken into the confidence of the authorities? What, in fact, was their role? The 2lst June 1940 issue of the 'Sussex Express' gave out a great deal of special information on what to do if the Germans came, mainly advising people to 'stay put', not to gossip and to leave the Home Defence forces to deal with the invasion. Those travelling were to obey instructions given to them by the police at road barriers. So, the basic policy regarding civilians was that they should 'stay put'.[33] The general public were on no account to leave their homes for some supposedly safer area and so start the mass refugee movement which had caused disaster in the Battle of France. It was this image which dominated the minds of the authorities. The rapid German movement across north east France in May had produced a tidal wave of civilians on foot with handcarts. The confusion had actually prevented British and French reinforcements from reaching the front and it was believed that the Germans deliberately used civilians as a cover for their movements. Hence, British civilians were to be persuaded that they would suffer less hardship and danger by remaining in their own neighbourhood.[34] A police directive of July 1942, but obviously summing up instructions over the previous two years, gives one pause to think. According to this, the civilian population was NOT supposed to adopt a purely passive role. The government expected the people to offer united opposition to an invader and every citizen should find means to hinder and frustrate the enemy; he should bring his ingenuity and common sense into play. For instance, stray parties of enemy soldiers presented a good opportunity and the government expected that 'every stout-hearted citizen would use all his power to overcome them'. This does sound rather inspiring but the precise methods to be used are not listed in detail. There does seem to be some contradiction here with previous instructions.[35]

The 'Stay Put' policy did not mean to say that civilians living in coastal areas could not move out *before* an invasion. The previous year, in July, the Hailsham Special Evacuation Committee had reported that Eastbourne schoolchildren were to be moved out. Arrangements were made for their registration in Hailsham. However, the mass movement envisaged did not actually take place, it seems. In the end, only two registered and these, finally, did not turn up. Hailsham itself was no longer encouraged to receive evacuees from London, and residents from Pevensey Bay, especially, were still being encouraged to move into Hailsham in September 1940. A weekly allowance of 5 shillings for adults and 3 shillings for children was authorised.[36] Eventually, this encouragement to move had some success, and residents can recall Eastbourne firms setting up shop in Hailsham. Cameron's and Plummer's were examples. However, this movement seems to have been a response more to severe bombing in Eastbourne in 1941 than to invasion scares.[37]

Of course, the minds of officials and the military were full of the dangers of invasion and they were anxious to safeguard the people. After all, fighting would involve the use of armoured vehicles and perhaps glider landings and parachute drops. These latter had been used successfully by the Germans in the Low Countries and in Denmark. Although we now know that the Germans had no plans to use this form of attack in England, the airborne troops were particularly feared during the early years of the War. It was this fast movement of troops and the chance of their unexpected appearance in unlikely places which gave such an emphasis to the control of civilian movement.

However, this is not to say that *very* local civilian movement was not envisaged. As far as the Triumvirate was concerned this would have to be planned for. People would have to be moved from one part of the Nodal Point to another when a particular building was required for military purposes or evacuated because they were in the line of fire. It was no use leaving this until the last minute. Such movements would have to be forecast and arrangements for their billeting and food supply made ahead.[38] In fact Miss Rous, who lived in Ersham Road, can distinctly remember receiving such a warning. It might be remembered that she lived just outside the Nodal Point and would therefore be in particular danger.[39]

In spite of the optimism of their propaganda, the authorities were willing to face the fact that the 'Stay Put' policy would probably not work. A military appreciation of the summer of 1940 looked at the problem from the point of view of military casualties. Lieutenant-Colonel C.W. Healey, the officer in charge of 190 Field Ambulance which covered the area inland from Pevensey Bay to Rye Bay, was particularly worried about 'Bungalow Town', in Pevensey Bay. One can hardly imagine the people in these rather flimsy homes waking up one morning to the sights and sounds of a German Armada appearing over the horizon, obeying the order to 'Stay Put'. The Lieutenant-Colonel realised that civilian casualties would probably be very heavy. He decided to evacuate civil and military wounded indiscriminately—but they would have to be re-

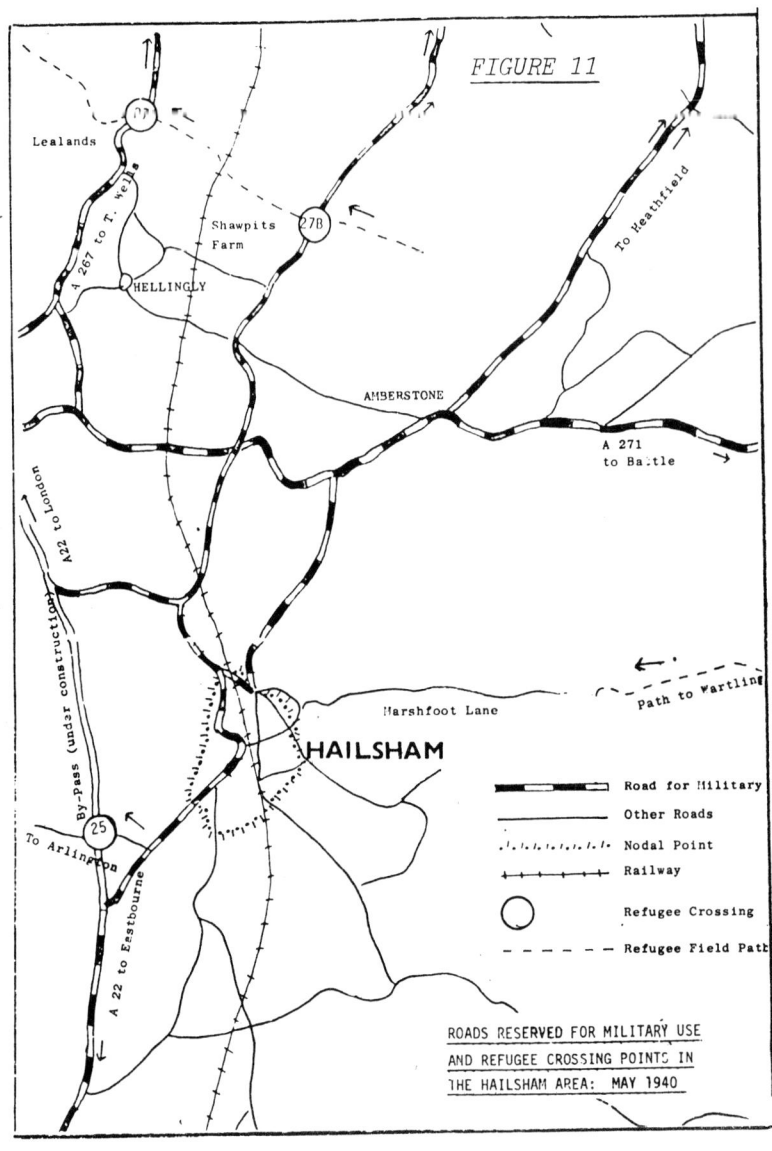

Roads reserved for Military Use and Refuge Crossing Points. May 1940

arranged according to severity of wounds and by sexes as soon as possible.[40]

The fact had to be faced then; whatever the official policy was, refugees would probably soon be on the move. As early as May 1940, plans were being made to deal with this. The Regional Commander issued police forces with an emergency instruction sheet firmly marked 'Secret'. According to this, it was hoped to reduce 'unorganised' evacuation to a minimum. It then immediately goes on to say:

> It is anticipated that the immediate effect of invasion on traffic will be two simultaneous movements:
> 1. The movement of large numbers of defending troops.
> 2. Unorganised evacuation by members of the public ...

Now, it was the job of the police to ensure the progress of traffic going up to the front using the main roads and especially those leading south. Civilian evacuation was intended to be mainly in a westerly direction. This traffic was intended to cross military routes only at certain specific points. The accompanying map (Figure 11) shows which roads were to be denied to civilians and where these crossing points were. It is quite clear that all main roads radiating from Hailsham were for military use only. In many cases, civilians were expected to travel by foot because the crossing points do not seem to envisage the use of metalled roads. For instance, the minor road from Windmill Hill to Pevensey was denied to them and refugees from the Norman's Bay area were expected to cross this road at Wartling. There is an east-west road leading from Hooe to Wartling. However, even on a fairly large scale map, there is no obvious footpath continuing west. Presumably, the field path leading from Coopers Farm in the general direction of New Bridge would have to do. This ultimately leads along the top of the embankment of Whelpley Sewer and joins up with Marshfoot Lane. Clearly, it would be helpful if the Germans invaded in summer. We can see a similar situation north-west of Hailsham. The crossing at the end of Arlington road, which leads in the general direction of Michelham Priory, is perfectly satisfactory for wheeled transport. This, however, is not the case in the Hellingly area. The A267, the Tunbridge Wells road through Horam, as well as the minor road west of Hellingly Hospital and leading towards

Marle Green were reserved for the Military but they could cross them by the lane leading to Shawpits Farm and Lealands. Again, this implies the use of field paths leading in a generally north-west direction. The route can be traced on the map through Gun Hill and Stream Farm, ultimately ending up in the general area of East Hoathly. It does seem that these refugees were expected to be absorbed into the countryside. This was not too bad for the hale and hearty, but one wonders about the sick and elderly.[41]

It is quite clear that by May 10th 1940, very detailed evacuation schemes were in existence and maps had been prepared. The Police had been kept up-to-date by the office of the Regional Commissioner where the plan had been instigated. It is, therefore, surprising to find the Tunbridge Wells headquarters denying much knowledge a week later when they wrote to Mr Martin at County Hall, Lewes, the man in charge of Civil Defence for the whole of East Sussex. Obviously, he had been asking for information about possible refugee movements. He was told that nothing more than tentative results could be given and that 'any maps which may be provided cannot possibly be kept up to date'. And yet, the letter written to the police a week prior to this was full of detailed amendments. For instance, the unclassified road from Windmill Hill to Pevensey had just been added to the list. The list itself had obviously been issued some time before May 10th and the copy still at the County Record Office shows that somebody has conscientiously crossed out certain roads and added others as alterations have arrived from Tunbridge Wells. These alterations have been pencilled in on a large scale map. It is clear that Civil Defence services were not allowed to be fully in the know. Although this letter goes on to say that regional control centres would do best to come to Regional Headquarters in an emergency if they wanted direction, it is difficult to imagine how Civil Defence could have functioned if refugees were on the move and communications had broken down.[42]

In the summer of 1940, the police, at least, were involved in the preparation of detailed schemes to deal with the civilian onrush. By the beginning of May they had already surveyed the roads in their respective divisions and prepared a large number of wooden signs to show prospective evacuation routes. Pinned onto these wooden signs were arrows roughly marked out on pieces of paper. Of course, these road signs were to show no indication of place names;

there were only arrows showing the general direction in which refugees were supposed to go. Road blocks were ready to be put into position.[43] It was made quite clear that the police would be unarmed; but nevertheless, it was expected that they would maintain public order. In fact, they were charged with the detection of 'treacherous or subversive activities.' Again, the fear of a Fifth Column is quite clear. Quite detailed instructions about crowd control were given, such as advisability of using responsible members of a group to obtain compliance.[44] Temporary police stations at refugee crossing points were also being set up. These were to be used mainly by Special Constables and provided washing and feeding facilities for them.

In fact, the enrolment of Specials was increasing considerably.[45] By February 1941, there were 9 of them in Hailsham itself[46] and Mrs D. White, who was living in Horsebridge at the time, remembers her father being sworn in early in the War. In September 1939, he was starting patrol duties in the area. He came into Hailsham for his course of instruction and worked with P.C. Hurd at Hellingly. He was quite clear that his duties under invasion conditions would involve keeping the main roads clear for military traffic 'and to shepherd the civilians onto side roads and bridleways'.[47] This shows that very detailed arrangements for refugee moves had been made. Nevertheless, the authorities were still in two minds about the situation. For instance, it was strongly emphasised that 'refugee signs must not be displayed until all efforts to restrain the public have failed and refugee traffic is well on the move'. The official policy was quite clear; but they knew it would fail. After all, their main efforts were clearly directed at dealing with 'panic evacuation' and not actually towards stopping the movement of people. Was the moment when the refugee signs came out an admission of defeat? There was no doubt about the movement of unauthorised *wheeled* traffic. 'Non-essential vehicles were to be turned into the fields and immobilised by smashing the distributor, deflating the tyres, removing the valve-locking nuts or by burning'.[48]

Meanwhile, the Triumvirate continued to prepare for Hailsham under siege throughout 1941. It was felt that First Aid Parties were fairly adequate. A great deal was based on the Church Room at Victoria Road but more work needed to be done to protect it. Other F.A.P.'s. were in the process of recruitment and particular attention was being paid to the needs of the population outside the Nodal Point. The Rescue Party, based at George Dann's Ltd, was gaining protected accommodation. The Decontamination Party was brought inside the perimeter.[49] A conference on the 19th February discussed the Casualty Reception Centre in the basement of Kirby Croft Chambers. This, too, needed reinforcement. There was a strong move to transfer all First Aid Stations from outside the Nodal Point to the Church Room or the Red Cross Headquarters in North Street.[50]

It is significant that the perimeter clearly goes out of its way to include the Common Pond and the small pond near the slaughterhouse. The main worry here seems to have been water supply for fire fighting. The Fire Brigade contained two pumping units and 5,500 feet of hose and was given a special allowance of 650 gallons of petrol. Its membership was felt to be well up to strength. A survey of shelters in midsummer suggests that practically the whole population had some sort of shelter available, public or private.[51] In March 1941 there were 30 A.R.P. members based on Mr George Dann's garage. However, 12 of them would have to sleep sitting up because there was not enough room. This accommodation was protected with sand bags and heavy timbers. It was hoped to partition off a section of the Church Room to give extra protection. However, opposition from the Vicar put a stop to this. In the end, it was decided to erect Anderson shelters in the hall.[52] By August 1941 there were 45 Shelter Wardens in the Rural District to help wardens. They were still in training at the time. It seems fairly clear that each member of the population had been allocated a shelter space and that each person knew which shelter to go to when the time came. There was even a reserve of strutted basements 'in case of an influx from outside'. The main problem was the state of some of the Anderson shelters. Far too many people in Hailsham seemed to think that the corrugated iron shell was in itself sufficient protection. Only a few of them had been covered with the required 30 inches of earth on the sides and 18 inches on the top. Householders were circulated with a warning letter from Mr Carr.[53] By the beginning of 1942 one begins to feel that the people of Hailsham were starting to lose enthusiasm for emergency preparations. They probably felt that the danger of invasion was now remote. In fact, U.S. forces were starting to arrive in England and the German Army was thoroughly occupied in Russia. There was difficulty in recruiting people for First Aid Parties and membership was 'fluctuating and uncertain'. Far from shoring up their Anderson shelters with earth, people were beginning to take these eyesores down.[54]

The importance of food supplies under emergency conditions is suggested by the fact that the Food Executive Officer was, in fact, Mr Carr himself by the beginning of 1941, although in this respect he was directly responsible to the Ministry of Food itself, not to the R.D.C.[55] Special emergency reserves were set up in various places. They were decentralised to ensure that the whole of the emergency supply was not wiped out one shell. In view of Hailsham's duty to last out for a week under siege without outside help, it was essential that the people could be fed.[56] In fact, the Food Officer could, during an emergency, requisition food, although receipts had to be given.[57] One of the places used in Hailsham for food storage was Southerden and Crowhurst in North Street. This was one of the few places in the town which escaped the blitz on railings made in the search for scrap metal. It was wondered why this shop should be an exception. In fact, they stayed there as a precaution against people looting the premises during a crisis. A great deal of effort was made to keep the location of this treasure house secret. One surviving food worker feels that, 'there was a great deal that people didn't know, and that it was wise for them not to know'.[58] If the Germans were about to invest the town then the Food Executive Officer had the right to destroy surplus food so that the enemy could not commandeer it. This created a problem with McDougall's Mill at Horsebridge. The only way of destroying flour was by blowing it up and arrangements were made with the Army to carry this out should it become necessary.[59] Meanwhile, the public was being told how to cook outdoors during an emergency.[60] Food production in the surrounding agricultural area received attention. It was vital that this should continue under invasion conditions and farmers were told to stay on their farms until the last possible moment. If the invasion were repelled, food production might become even more important. Consequently, crops and cattle should not be destroyed unless orders were given by the Military.[61]

The Triumvirate was bombarded with instructions from the Ministry of Health about water supply. The Food Organiser was responsible for this as well. He was supposed to work on the basis of two gallons per person per day. Throughout recorded history, water supply has, of course, been the crucial problem for the besieged. A 20th century society requires not just water, but pure water. Water Squads had to be put together in order to organise distribution after a probable disruption of the mains. This was especially the case with Hailsham, which drew its supplies from outside the Nodal Point. The Water Squad had to seek new sources of water, see to the chlorinating and dechlorinating of water in the tanks and organise the issuing of water to the public, who were supposed to bring their own receptacles and carry the water away. Meanwhile, the Ministry of Health was willing to provide facilities from their own laboratory at Horsham for bacteriological examination. Wells, of course, need opening up and cleaning out and it was suggested that the Water Squads should make use of any galvanised iron tanks lying around the countryside for storage and collection. It was pointed out, however, that expenditure should he kept to a minimum.[62] A report involving Mr Carr in June 1941 envisages a supply of 11,000 gallons a day for an inner perimeter population of 2,500—more than 4 gallons per capita; this was twice as much as that suggested by the Ministry of Health. Hailsham was generously supplied with wells which could easily be made available. The best was at the rear of the R.D.C. offices at Cortlandt. Sufficient receptacles for storage and transport had been gathered by this time.[63]

Damage caused to water supplies and sewers was likely to cause problems of sanitation. As soon as an attack commenced, the use of W.C's. and baths was to stop. Commodes, buckets or trench latrines were envisaged.[64]

Hence, by mid-1941, Hailsham was fully prepared for German investment. For 10 days, it could hope to hold out against the enemy and be self-sufficient. But by then, the crisis was over. Britain could still be defeated at sea but there would be no invasion and people knew this. Preparations, once started, must have continued under their own momentum. The lack of evidence of detailed plans before early 1941 is still a puzzle. Only the problem of refugees seems to have been seriously considered in the summer of 1940. Lack of written evidence does not automatically imply lack of action. Nevertheless, the tone of the early 1941 correspondence does suggest radically new thought about the problem: furthermore, Hailsham was certainly not unique in this respect.

CHAPTER FOUR
'There was a plane and I could see something falling...'

As usual, we are wiser than the planners of the past. We can look at the organisers of Civil Defence during the pre-war and 'Phoney War' period and actually see them making their mistakes. Of course, we know what happened. They did not know what was going to happen. They had little evidence to go on, and what little evidence they had was often misleading. The experience of bombing during the First World War bore little relation to the new scale of possibilities. Only 300 tons of bombs were dropped on this country before 1918 and fewer than 2,000 people were killed. The legend that 'the bomber will always get through' was, by the late 1930's, a very powerful one. This image was augmented by the devastation caused by air bombing during the Spanish Civil War by a relatively small number of German squadrons. It must be remembered that the raids in Spain were daylight affairs and victims were out in the open. The fear of bombing played no small part in the government's 'appeasement' policy in the pre-war years, and on the outbreak of war, the authorities were prepared for immediate massive bombing offensives. Actual invasion was hardly thought about at this stage. This probably helps to explain the initial concentration in Sussex on Civil Defence against air attack as opposed to preparations to meet an invasion.[1] The detailed planning for Civil Defence arose from rather exaggerated fears of widespread air bombardment and gas attacks.

At the outbreak of war, most of the responsibility for Civil Defence was carried out by the County rather than the Rural District and Local organisation came through County Divisions. The attitude of Hailsham towards Civil Defence before the Munich crisis was one of rampant apathy. There was no training, and few volunteers were coming forward. The authorities stated that they 'had the matter in hand', and added, rather mysteriously, that they would try new methods to get volunteers. People seemed to think that it was all the responsibility of the County Medical Officer, but he denied any knowledge of this. There was vague talk about people being selected for Decontamination Squads but it was feared that they would, in the event, be used for road or rescue gangs. The overlapping of functions was a headache for all concerned. The A.R.P was still far more a County than a District interest. They had reached the stage of supplying each warden with a six inch map and A.R.P. badges.

By April 1939 it was decided that the Rural District should be aiming at eight first Aid Parties and twelve ambulances with eight cars for sitting casualties. Fifty one drivers, mostly women, had already been recruited. There was certainly by this time, a Mobile First Aid Post located at Hellingly Hospital. By June, there were four first Aid Depots in the District. In Hailsham, Dr Shaw was the Medical Officer of the mobile unit—a 15 cwt. van belonging to Green Brothers who were making the fittings.[2] Things were beginning to move. There was even a Decontamination Party ready for action. By the outbreak of war the town had a full-time A.R.P. officer and a Fire Officer, both paid £250 a year.[3] However, the sense of urgency, detectable in the records, was rather defused by a talk at the Hailsham Rotary Club, which took place at 'The George' in August 1939. It described a recent visit to Germany by a 'Sussex Express' reporter. He emphasised the welcome he received and an 'absence of irksome restrictions'.[4] Nevertheless, the A.R.P. Committee was less complacent. The A.R.P. Controller, Major C.H. Alexander,C.B.E., resigned in disgust at the lack of co-operation inside the Council. He was worried that there was still only one Decontamination Squad and that the organisation of the Hailsham Control Room was getting nowhere. Mr Keith Martin, who later became a Billeting Officer, and then the Chairman of the Civil Defence Committee, was also dissatisfied. Major Alexander resumed duties immediately on the outbreak of war. Mr. A.S. Boniface was appointed Head Warden and was very busy fitting respirators onto schoolchildren.[5]

By December there were more than a hundred members of the various First-Aid Parties. There were also approximately 50 drivers of various sorts of vehicle. The Decontamination Squads were well up to establishment but there were no Rescue Parties as yet. There was a huge number of wardens, 348 altogether in the Rural District, and two thirds of these were fully trained. The Control

Room seems to have been fully staffed although there was, as yet, a shortage of messengers. Obviously, a great deal of energy had been displayed in a short time.[6] However, the wave of enthusiasm for A.R.P. was not as overwhelming as it looked. As late as March 1940 we find opposition in Hailsham to the idea of Civil Defence lectures on Sundays.[7]

On September 2nd 1939 the R.D.C. held meeting at Cortlandt in solemn anticipation of the outbreak of War. In fact, this was the last such meeting at the R.D.C. office as the premises were needed by the A.R.P. In future, Council meetings were to take place at Downford, next door.[8] In fact, this represents the beginning of Cortlandt as a proper Control Centre. The emergence of local Control Centres at this period represents the growth of the Districts as Civil Defence Authorities. These centres had a crucial role to play. In a typical emergency the process would be started off by the local warden, who would be first on the scene, filling in a message form. This would immediately be telephoned to the Control Centre where incidents would be plotted on a map. Here a decision would be made as to how much and what type of Civil Defence service was needed. The Centre would then telephone First Aid Posts and Depots, Rescue Parties and ambulances.[9] A typical situation is described in 'H:A.R.P', a monthly newsletter produced by the Hailsham A.R.P. for wardens in the area:

> SCENE. The peaceful countryside and an 'Alert' is in operation. TIME. 15.00 hours. 'BANG! BANG! BANG!'
> 'Those were close; must be in my area'. Warden dons his helmet and hurries out. Rising smoke, glare in the sky and information from passers-by indicates trouble at Cowbarn Farm, Haildron. On the way occasional short blasts on whistle will mobilise local stirrup pump Fire Parties.
> 15.05. —Warden arrives on scene. Rapidly investigates and finds as follows:
> 3 H.E. and some I.B's fallen. Farmhouse partly wrecked. Casualties serious and minor, 2 persons trapped. FIRE. Road partly blocked. Water mains broken. Overhead electric cables damaged.
> 15.10. —FIRST DUTY is to send an EXPRESS REPORT to Hailsham Sub-Control thus:
> ––Telephone Hailsham 313/314.

EXPRESS REPORT
Wardens' Post X.3. Warden Smith.
3 H.E. and some I.B. at Haildron.
1500 hours.
Some casualties.
NEXT DUTY—Call Services.[10]

Miss Knowles remembers working in the Control Room during the early part of the War. It was, in fact, the old Council Chamber shored up with enormous timber beams. The Clerk to the Council was the Chief Controller. During the daytime he was in charge. At night, various Assistant Controllers, such as Major Alexander and Colonel Johnson, were fully responsible and they slept in a small upstairs room. Day and night the Control Room was manned by a team of volunteers on twelve hour shifts and it was their job to attend to the four telephones. Miss Knowles remembers that at her shift they often played Mah Jong to keep themselves awake. This went on for five years during which time they were actually disturbed very little. During the daytime Miss Knowles worked in the office of the Chief Warden in Downford. When Mr. Ralph Ricardo took over his job he produced the H.A.R.P. magazine and she did the typing.[11]

A thousand pounds was spent on the protection of the Control Room and the various sandbags and trenches outside. What with this and the increase in rates there was a certain amount of public muttering.[12] A fair amount of cash went on petrol supplies—rationed by this time. In view of this, the Civil Defence services were quite generous. For instance, the A.R.P. were allowed 74 gallons a month and the rescue services 32 gallons. Complaints began to be heard. The most important controversy centred on the lack of air raid shelters for schoolchildren. The heavy expenditure, especially that involving the R.D.C. buildings, was resented when the children at Battle Road school were expected to shelter in corridors during raids.[13] The Control Room was always short of staff—partly due to the needs of the armed forces. In fact, there seems to have been a persistent problem of competition between Civil Defence and Home Guard for personnel at a time when manpower was critically scarce. The form sent out by Regional Headquarters on the very day of Eden's request for L.D.V. volunteers shows considerable anxiety. All the Sub-Controls in East Sussex were telephoned by Regional Control within half an hour. It seems that it was acceptable for men under military age and those with army training to join the new organisation; the danger was that fully trained wardens might be poached by the L.D.V.[14]

Another problem was that the Civil Defence services tended to lose their trained personnel because numbers of the part-time volunteers were losing their employment, and, on registering at the Employment Exchange were liable to be sent to any part of the country under the Emergency Labour Regulations. The difficulty was especially acute with fire and rescue services. The Emergency Committee hinted that the L.D.V. had considerably more glamour than Civil Defence: 'the number of persons available for recruitment has been greatly reduced since the formation of the Local Defence Volunteer Corps'.[15] When all allowance has been made for these problems, however, there was still a certain amount of apathy to overcome. For instance, the Methodist minister gave a stiff sermon on the need for staff for First Aid and A.R.P.[16] During July 1940, at the height of the invasion scare, the churches still saw themselves as important media for social control and had obviously agreed to follow this line as well. During this period the Vicar was asking in the Parish Magazine for more volunteers. This had been suggested to him by Captain Gardner:

> ...there may still be in Hailsham persons who might be available and there must be many other persons in the surrounding hamlets which are well served by buses who could come forward and help ... That wise old man, Aesop, ... gave us the fable of the little mouse eating away the net to rescue the lion. Thank God, the British Lion is not yet in a net but he needs all his little mice to help him and that is YOU and ME.[17]

The Emergency Committee of the R.D.C. met 20 times during the month of September 1939. One of the main topics for discussion seems to have been air raid warnings. By the outbreak of war Hailsham's siren had been installed in Green Brothers' factory. This was provided by the Council at the cost of £9.10.0. and Green's paid for the cost of fitting and the motor. Immediately the Prime Minister's broadcast announcing the outbreak of war was finished, the siren in Hailsham went into action. The result was that the population in the streets rushed into the Control Room. This caused considerable confusion and so a shelter was built for 50 people outside the Council Offices. Apparently, this was based on an out-of-date pattern. The County A.R.P. Officer inspected this in mid-October and expressed severe disapproval.[18] There was also a distinct problem about the siren at Green's. In January 1940 the Regional Officer recommended that it should be transferred to the Police Station. However, it was still at Green's in February when a test was made. When it was in the same place in May, the situation seems to have been accepted for good.[19] By August 1940 and for the next few months, the siren came into its own. The Battle Road School log book records warnings nearly every other day after September 16th and there were 40 in all before the end of the Autumn term.[20]

Meanwhile, Civil Defence activity continued in Hailsham. In May 1940 a 22 seater charabanc was bought for £50 to serve as a First Aid Post and the records detail such events as Mr Gutsell's willingness to act as cycle messenger provided the Council was willing to pay 8 shillings for a lamp. There were also, by now, 27 unofficial parties of builders willing to perform as Rescue Parties.[21] After the summer of 1940 comparisons become difficult because of the concentration on Hailsham as a Nodal Point. The Civil Defence requirements to deal with ground attack were very different from those connected with air raids. After all, Hailsham had never been a prime target for bombing. However, in the event of invasion, the town could have suffered very severely indeed. The point is that the records now tend to deal with the zone inside the defended perimeter, an area much smaller than the Rural District. The population referred to was a mere 2,500 instead of the District's 34,000. The actual statistics, then, are based on quite different criteria.

The more formal documents, such as the R.D.C. minutes, and those of its various committees, as well as the Civil Defence reports, are useful as a framework for which the investigator is thankful. However, oral and written memories, although less reliable in terms of precise dates and figures, help us to understand what it was like for those actually involved. There is considerable interest in looking at these types of evidence together and testing them against each other. For instance, Mr Pitcher remembers as a schoolboy the feeling of mounting urgency. He recalls Mr Chamberlain's return from Munich with his 'piece of paper'. The 'peace in our time' aspect of it all coincided, ironically, with increasing pressure to participate in Civil Defence. Sometime in 1938 there was a trial blackout when all house windows had to be covered and street lights put out. Mr Pitcher remembers both of his parents going out on patrol as Wardens for the first time that night to see that no lights were showing. It was during this period that they were attending lectures on first aid and how to secure a house against gas attack. There was a great deal of talk about the Spanish Civil War.[22]

Although women were expressly forbidden to be armed and could not therefore join the Home Guard, nevertheless they had close links with both Civil Defence organisations. They manned Rest Centres and Clothing Centres, drove Mobile Canteens and cared for bomb victims. In May 1940 the W.V.S. started the village Messenger service in East Sussex which involved more than 4,000 women. Eventually this developed into the official Civil Defence Messenger Service. Their after-care duties involved more than just standing around after a raid. They were allowed to display a blue window-card showing that they were prepared to provide hot drinks and blankets for casualties at a moment's notice.[23]

The daily life of the A.R.P. service is well illustrated by Miss Knowles' memories of driving about the countryside in a rather disreputable old van. One of her jobs was to deliver equipment to the various wardens' posts. Miraculously, this survived repeated journeys loaded with sandbags, mainly to various pubs, it seems. The customers were quite happy to display a kind of reverse male chauvinism, ignoring the ladies struggling in with sand bags. If they were in uniform, they were not perceived as needing help. The little van was also responsible for delivering hundreds of tin hats around the district, as well as countless unsorted shoes and large mattresses which hung over the tailboard and catch light from the exhaust.[24]

The whole Civil Defence system revolved around the ordinary warden. Regarded with suspicion during the 'Phoney War' period with his obsessions about chinks of light showing, he came into his own once the bombs began to fall. It was his job to judge the extent and severity of bomb damage and to organise the smooth running of first aid and rescue. For instance, he had to be able to tell Rescue Parties which bodies, alive or dead, might be under the debris—and where. This he could only do by knowing his neighbourhood and its people intimately, and by earning their confidence. Many wardens were, in fact, women, and the experiences of Miss Knowles are by no means untypical.[25]

Mr Salvage joined the Civil Defence in 1938 as an Auxiliary Fireman. However, because he was living at the bottom of Elmsdown Place at the time it was felt that he would be more useful as a warden. His area embraced Stoney Lane, Elmsdown Place, Garfield Road and Bellbanks Road. Mr Salvage and his colleague, Arthur Keeley, split the night duties between them so that they could have alternate nights off. Even so, it was still tiring with a full day's work. Mr Salvage worked at Knight's Nurseries which at that time was producing vegetables as quickly as it could. His first job as a Warden was to distribute gas masks:

> I used to go around fitting the little Mickey Mouse masks for youngsters. My daughter loved her Mickey Mouse and she used to go round with me as some children had trouble with them. I found it was good psychology as she would pop hers on and then other children would pop theirs on too ...[26]

Mr Salvage was drilled in decontamination methods and he mentions the Decontamination Chamber in Hailsham. This was a building in the Vicarage Field area designed for the special purpose of treating any gas casualties. There was also a Cleansing Station in North Street which was completed in 1941. This was a brick building with six compartments and clothing was to be removed in the adjoining lean-to. In the first compartment eyes were washed and in the second there were showers. In the third, fresh clothing would be supplied. There were, of course, separate facilities for either sex. With the chamber went 14 defence workers and a supervisor. Instruction classes were carried out in the Church Room under Dr Shaw. Hailsham had, by this time,[27] also gained some sort of facility for decontaminating clothing. This emphasises the problems associated with Mustard Gas in particular which tended to be slow to dissolve, especially if sprayed in liquid form, and caused severe burns to the skin. Clothing exposed to it had to be cleansed before it could be worn again.[28] Mr Roberts spent a great deal of time at the beginning of the War checking that people were carrying their gas masks but later on, he remembers, they stopped bothering.[29] Even the sight of the Hailsham Auxiliary Fire Service playing darts in gas masks failed to rally enthusiasm.[30]

Instructions came to the wardens through Mr Ricardo, the Chief Warden. He used to start work at his Office next door to Cortlandt in the early morning and was lucky to get home at 10 p.m.

As incendiary bombs grew more frequent, there was increasing emphasis on stirrup pump drill.[31] Every street was encouraged to have sand and stirrup pumps available and householders, it was suggested, should make sure that it was easy to gain entry to their homes. The Head Warden believed that there should be one fire-watcher in every house.[32] Lt. Col. Gwynne, Chairman of the R.D.C., was concerned with the nature of large fires created by enemy raiders as a means of guiding in bombers with high explosives:

> It is every citizen's duty immediately to render harmless any incendiary bomb that falls near him and I ask all householders, employers and shopkeepers to co-operate with the Civil Defence Service.[33]

Mr Salvage had the inevitable duty of checking on lights. People, he insists, were co-operative about this and, on one occasion at least, were willing to report their neighbours to the police for leaving blackout curtains open. He was entitled to break into a house if people were out and the lights were showing.[34] Searle's, the drapers in the High Street, were doing a brisk trade in blackout curtains, especially after the first blackout practice in August 1939.[35] All this gave rise to problems. People obviously had difficulty in finding their way about and methods were suggested of treating house name-plates with luminous paint and using masked torches to find one's way home in the dark. More serious was the increase in road accidents due to the restrictions on vehicle headlights.[36]

Mr Salvage recalls a typical wartime story with no satisfactory ending. When there was nothing particular to do on duty he would drop in at the fire watchers' post at the gasholder for a warm at their fire. On one occasion during the Autumn of 1940 a light sprang up on the marshes just as enemy planes were crossing the coast. At first they thought that somebody was being careless but when it happened four nights in a row they began to feel that someone might be signalling to the enemy. After a while a brilliant idea occurred to him:

> I went and got a camera tripod with an octopod piece on the top with a universal joint, clamped a piece of copper tubing to it, jammed the tripod on the ground with a clear view down to the marsh and the next time the light came it kept on for a full

minute. I turned the copper tubing so that I got it in the range of the tube so that I could look through it and see the light. The police came down and it was reported to the military. Later on I met one of the constables who had first seen the light with me and asked him about it. He looked at me and said, 'Well, they got 'em'; and that's all they ever did say.[37]

As usual, the air of secrecy was very pervasive and all the Civil Defence services were warned not to talk about their duties.[38]

A fair amount of Mr Ricardo's time must have been spent producing the H.A.R.P. circular which sometimes ran for as much as 20 pages. The editions for September and October 1941 have fortunately survived and give a good general impression of A.R.P. life. Copies are labelled, 'for limited circulation only', and readers are warned that they must be returned within three weeks. The September number contains a competition, for a reward of a hundred cigarettes, for the best report on an imaginary situation, which is described in some detail. The opening section has already been referred to and it is worth studying carefully as it gives a thorough run-down on most of the Civil Defence services. The story goes on to describe the arrival of the Rescue Party because trapped casualties are in danger of fire. The First Aid Party also arrives promptly. The Warden himself was not supposed to do any detailed work but to remain on the spot in charge of the incident 'in a conspicuous position'. In due course a messenger and various neighbours turn up and they are detailed to do such useful work as traffic control—vehicles must have somewhere to park without getting in each other's way—or keeping people away from fallen electric cables. There were cups of tea to give to minor casualties and fingers had to be applied to pressure points until the First Aid Party could turn its attention to bleeding. Pending the arrival of the Fire Brigade, Stirrup Pump Parties had to be set to work. At odd moments, the Warden would start filling in his interim report.

During the War the Hailsham Mobile First Aid Post was run from Dr Shaw's house, St Wilfrid's, at 72 High Street. At all times there were three or four nurses on duty there. They attended 28 incidents altogether. It is worth emphasising the rather unique dedication of such services in a little-bombed rural area. There must have been long periods of boredom when nothing much happened; but they had to maintain a state of readiness. In all, 124,656 hours of service were put in.[39] In 1940, 21 Red Cross members were attached to the Hailsham First Aid Post for standby duties of eight hours a day. Thirteen of these had qualified for war service stripes during the first year of the War. However, those on duty at Dr Shaw's were not necessarily all members of the Red Cross. The whole strength of the detachment was, at times, nearly 50.[40] Dr Shaw and his wife, a qualified nurse, did a great deal of the actual training. He seems to have been quite willing for his house to become a dormitory, with the men in one living room and the women in rooms upstairs. He went out with the Mobile Unit himself and vividly recalls an occasion at one of the outlying farms when they found four people sitting up in bed, apparently uninjured, but quite dead from the effects of blast. The odd thing was that two glass decanters by the bedside were unaffected.[41] Mr Salvage remembers Dr Shaw's prompt intervention after a serious bomb incident in 1943. Within a few moments of the warning being given, the Mobile Unit had arrived with its team and the Fleur de Lys was set up as a medical station. By the time that trapped victims were brought in by the Rescue Party, Dr Shaw had already treated two patients who had been injured on the street.[42]

Mrs Burgess, of Summerheath Road, joined the Red Cross in 1941, although she had previously received training. She had less fear of the darkness in wartime than she has now. Her shift at St Wilfrid's started at 10 p.m. although there were enough volunteers for her duty to come around only once a fortnight.[43] The Divisional Superintendent of St John's, Mr A.J. Burgess, recalls a flurry of training in Civil Defence just before the outbreak of war. The Brigade seems to have been heavily involved in the training of the public to replace St John's members who were called up. People in the Brigade seem to have been on call at their homes, rather like those in the Auxiliary Fire Service, and had to report to their headquarters in Grovelands Road during an emergency. This H.Q. was continuously manned. In early 1941 their First Aid Centre was established at the Church Rooms in Victoria Road and the ambulances were garaged at 'The George'.[44] Some of the St John's members, such as as Mr Ted Marchant, became members of Rescue Groups. Members of these were mainly builders or demolition experts, it was useful for them to contain trained first aid members for the treatment of trapped victims. This particular Rescue Party was situated where Sturton Place is and Mr Marchant recalls the fully fitted-out ambulance with an aluminium top and provision for two stretchers.⁴⁵

With the medical services, there was considerable room for confusion with overlapping and intercrossing personnel and organisations, some of which had long-standing corporate identities. As with most Civil Defence work, the basic integration was carried out by the Local Authority, in this case the A.R.P. Committee of the R.D.C. They appointed Mr Funnell, from St John's, as commandant of the First Aid Party, and Dr Shaw as Medical Officer for the Mobile Unit in June 1939. The Committee was instrumental in procuring various vehicles for the Mobile Units, although Dr Shaw put his foot down when it was suggested that a bicycle would do for messages: a motor cycle was essential. By November 1940, the Unit had a full-time driver at £3.5.0 a week. The Committee also had an important role in finance. For example, Dr Shaw was granted 5 shillings a week during winter months for the cost of lighting and heating the sleeping quarters at St Wilfrid's. They even paid for the cost of new hot water bottles.⁴⁶

As the war progressed and places like Hailsham were seen as possible targets for direct assault by enemy invading troops, the tone of Civil Defence documents began to change. From now on, 100 per cent protection had to be provided for the civil population regardless of their financial situation. Great care had to be taken in the siting of shelters away from prominent landmarks such as churches and main road intersections. Standards of strength and waterproofing were much more strongly insisted on.⁴⁷ Meanwhile, Hailsham seemed to take great pride in its 'specimen shelter' in the garden of Downford. The trench was ten feet long and accommodated 4-6 people. 'It was lined with corrugated iron and an oil drum was sunk into the bottom of the trench to make a water sump.⁴⁸

On July 17th 1940, the Hailsham area was subjected to its first bombs. Seven high explosives were dropped on Cralle Place, Cowbeech, causing craters 5 feet deep.(49) Major Batten kept a detailed record in his diary:

> ... A plane flew over—dull-looking—didn't take any notice. Then it turned back; so I said, 'what's it doing?', Taylor, one of the men, said, 'one of ours, sir'. After another five minutes it came back again so he said, 'where's it been then?' I said, 'well, it's gone over the other side, bombed the Jerries and come back again'. It came back a fourth time and I saw little

objects come from under and swing from side to side. I said, 'my God, he's bombing us; come in here you silly old devil'. Taylor was standing on a muck heap saying, 'look at those!' We dived into the stack yard and cuddled down under some stacks because we thought we were safe there. The bombs screamed as they came. They skimmed across the top of the house, missing the chimney by about twenty or thirty feet. The first one dropped in Barnard's garden. He was a bit deaf and was sitting reading the paper in his house and he thought he heard the lorry backfire. It fell in the middle of his special rose bed—all the roses were deposited in my field. I think this German spotted one of our big fattening sheds for chickens— he thought they were military installations and made a shot at them.[50]

One of Major Batten's neighbours, an old lady, complained to the police about aircraft with black crosses on buzzing her whilst she was up a ladder picking apples.[51]

The summer of 1940 seems to have marked a change in attitude. According to the Major, people had seen the war up to that time 'as a rather exciting football game'. Had they found a German airman they would quite likely, he feels, have invited him in for a cup of tea. Their ideas changed when they began to see the damage caused by war.[52]

Hailsham itself was by no means a target area although it was tempting for bombers to aim at the railway station if they were on their way back home from London and they had a few bombs left. A stick of four bombs reached the railway line on August 16th, but none of them exploded immediately. A small section of Green Brothers' Factory was damaged but not enough to stop work. The only casualty was in the brick field in Station Road where a youth was killed when a delayed action bomb went off. Mr Roberts remembers one of these bombs dropping just as he arrived at work in Green Brothers'. He leapt off his bicycle and ran to a field to lie down.[53] Mr Salvage gives us rather more detail about this incident. It was a foggy day. He had just finished repairing Knight's Nursery. He was working in an open-fronted shed and behind him there were about 20 tons of anthracite. He had just left work and had got as far as the railway arch when a bomb dropped in the middle of the pile of coal:

You never saw such a cloud of dirt and dust in your life. We spent the next day trying to collect all the anthracite together ... but no one was hurt and I don't think anyone was worried.[54]

Miss Rous, living in Ersham Road, had a rather different experience with one of the same stick of bombs:

> I'd just got home from work and my mother had friends to tea and was going to give it to them in the garden. They'd seen the planes go over so they removed everything into the dining room ... and I said to my mother, although I could hear the planes, 'I wouldn't bother, it's all over'. I went out to the dining room door and there was a plane and I could see something falling. I went in again very quickly and we all got under the table. One bomb fell in the garden of Number 11 and Number 13 and one at the bottom of the garden over the wall which was Nursery property. The other one fell in Windsor Road and set the gas main alight. Apart from a few ceilings down they didn't do much damage. It upset our tea party though. I'd lived in Ersham Road since 1930 and it was the first time everyone went out into the road and talked to each other.[55]

The largest number of fatal casualties happened on November 2nd 1940 on a wet Saturday night when a bomb dropped behind a crowded bus at Rushlake Green. The bus was hurled over a hedge and fell on its side in a field. Five of the passengers and the conductor were killed.[56]

Hailsham Civil Defence, then, prepared for a great deal but, in the event, had comparatively little to cope with. The more humdrum restrictions of wartime life will be dealt with in the next chapter.

CHAPTER FIVE

'Don't you know there's a war on?'

Britain during the war years can only be described as a sort of democratic dictatorship. The extension of government control over the lives of ordinary individuals was accepted in view of the gravity of the War situation. This, however, did not prevent complaints and evasions and a certain amount of this emerges from the sources of the period.

The whole area of Food Control seems to illuminate the problems of the time. The Food Control officer in Hailsham at the start of the War was Mr Faulkner. There was an element of cryptography in his receipt of a telegram saying 'Government Absolute Priority' ... and then, 'Priority Local Food Executive Officer, Rural District Council Offices, Hailsham, Sussex. *Determined Food Keeper, London'*. This was the pre-arranged signal to form a Food Office. On 2nd September a special Council meeting was held and a Food Planning Committee chaired by Archdeacon Reid was formed.[1] There were 10 people on this Committee, 5 representing consumers and 5 for the tradesmen. Rationing did not start immediately as a great deal of preliminary work had to be done. One of the first jobs was to register all the retailers and catering establishments. All of these had to apply to the Committee to get licences to sell particular foods, otherwise they would get no supplies. The Committee seems to have kept an eye on people attempting to hoard food—it was an offence to buy more than one week's supply.[2]

Meanwhile, ration books and identity cards were being hastily prepared. These became the two vital documents through which government control of civilians was exercised. The first ration books were issued from Victoria Hall on 11th September. At length, Kirby Croft Chambers was given over completely to this job, as well as 'Yarra Yarra', a large house in North Street. A great many extra staff were taken on, most of them young girls. Mrs D

Walker was one of these. She remembers that about 33,000 ration books for the Hailsham District were issued every six months. Reference leaves had to be filled in. These were taken from old books to give details, so that a new one could be issued. One very large family with a great many relations caused Mrs Walker considerable problems. One of the members filled them up for the others using her own name each time. All the queries were thrown into a huge box called 'the odds and sods' and a Sunday morning was given over to sorting them out. Her husband, Mr Lou Walker, was in charge of processing the books and both he and Mr Faulkner worked until 10 pm on some nights as well as Sundays. The first batch of ration books was given out by the ever-available W.V.S. from files provided by the Registrar General and issued during January 1940. Identity cards were issued as the same time. The first occasion on which housewives took their newly printed ration books shopping was on Monday 8th January.[3] At first, only bacon and ham, 4 ounces per person per week, sugar (12 ounces) and butter (4 ounces) were covered. Meat went on ration in March, but fish remained unrationed, although difficult to find. Rationing began to bite in July when tea was included and before long the rations settled down at about 2 ounces of cooking fat and butter and about 4 ounces of margarine a week. In 1941 cheese and preserves followed but the amount varied from season to season.[4] The Committee was willing to top this up with permits for anyone who was able to furnish proof of having bought fruit for preserving purposes by letting them have extra sugar. This was welcomed by the W.I. in particular.[5] There are reports of black market activities in the Hailsham area, but the whole subject is very difficult to pin down.

The Committee seems to have served a useful purpose, standing as it did between the Food Office and the public. They knew the people in the district well and could sort out a complaint without bothering the Ministry. They were bombarded with requests for licences to trade and issued more than a thousand in the Hailsham area alone. Seventy four catering establishments applied, but many were rejected. These included two W.I.'s, two cricket clubs and one child welfare centre.[6] In August 1940 the W.I. complained that it was impossible to get a ration of tea for their meetings.[7]

Each individual had to register with a retailer. Customers had free choice in this but the retailer could refuse them. If the customer became dissatisfied with his shop then he could apply to the Committee for permission to change. This could cause problems when the person's true reason for wanting to move was because he owed the grocer some money. Regulations issued in July 1941 were rather hard on shops with fewer than 25 customers. Reasons given for this were that petrol, labour and customers' time would be saved. There was certainly a drift to larger shops by the public.[8]

All retailers had the monthly headache of collecting up the little coupons from the ration books and returning them to the Food Office. On the basis of this, orders were given to the wholesalers to provide the correct amount of food. Naturally the shopkeepers got things wrong at times, but the food Office was willing to issue permits ahead of time in order to prevent bottlenecks even though it was against the regulations. Some retailers, it seems, could be relied on not to take advantage when the rules were bent in their favour; others were less trustworthy and had to be treated according to the letter of the law. There was only one case, however, of a shopkeeper deliberately defrauding the public in the Rural District and he was prosecuted.

For most shopkeepers, the rationing period was a dreary, sticky nightmare. There were huge numbers of instructions and provisions which he couldn't hope to understand. He was short-staffed and all the counting of coupons had to be done at night when he was tired. The Food Office grew accustomed to the monthly returns being hopelessly wrong or unwittingly illegal. It was a simple matter to telephone the retailer and tell him that the Home Office was altering the returns to comply with regulations; in this way bureaucracy showed its human face. One retailer was always miraculously correct in his returns—except for tea. This worried him, of course: 6 or 12 pounds seemed to vanish every month. Mr Faulkner asked when the next delivery was to take place and went to his shop to spot what was happening. There were two entrances and each one was picketed. When the delivery man came in with the tea, he would wait until the shopkeeper had finished counting them and then exit through the rear with one or two packets still left on his barrow. The poor shopkeeper was too honest himself to have suspected such goings-on.

There had to be enough leeway in the system to meet sudden emergencies. Troop trains, for instance, might suddenly arrive at the Station or a whole division could turn up in the town without warning. On such occasions, a round-up of the shops had to be made and the necessary forms filled in later. Itinerants were always a problem. There were several judges on circuit in the area and they needed temporary cards. These did not always catch up with the judge and again the law needed bending a little. One is relieved to learn that judges were comparatively honest in this respect. We get the impression of a meticulous scheme drawn up in Whitehall to meet every contingency. There was no way in which this could be realised in practice and the Food Office was quite happy to adapt regulations to reality.[9]

Mrs D. White suggests that people living in the country had considerable advantages over town dwellers. All sorts of thrifty habits were in common use anyway, even without rationing. Her family was able to rely on home-grown fruit and vegetables and always produced their own eggs. These were preserved from the flush spring period to be eaten in winter. Fruit was bottled in Kilner jars and preservation was perfectly good in water instead of in syrup. Mrs White stresses that this sort of farmhouse people were used to making do for themselves and that they carried on in the same way as usual, adapting to the new war conditions where necessary. Soap was never used from the shops but always left to harden for six months. In this way, it did not disappear so quickly. However, making briquettes of coal-dust was something new. The dust was dampened, mixed with a little cement and pressed into small moulds to dry.[10]

At this time, there were constant references to rationing in the newspapers. Each edition of the Sussex Express had a column entitled 'Home Notes' and dealt with the housewife's concerns. Yeast was suggested for use in cakes to cut down the need for sugar. A vegetable pie is mentioned as well as hints on cooking sheeps' heads. There are suggestions for bottling fruit with Campden fruit preserving tablets. Methods of making Christmas cakes without eggs are described. Poaching was one logical response to the meat shortage and the Press mentions a case in the Hailsham Petty Sessions in January 1941. The accused said that they had been unable to eat meat for a fortnight and that they could see nothing wrong in poaching, especially as they had a large family. In the August 22nd edition, Charles Diplock advertises that he is willing to buy fat horses fit for human consumption. There was an appeal in the same month for farmers to allow 'properly organised groups' to pick blackberries on their land. It was anticipated that there would be parties of schoolchildren, Scouts and Guides. A recipe with the rather sinister name *appelkraut*, unadvisedly published in June 1941, was not very well received and there was a letter to the effect that 'British people would not, at this time, wish to gain a taste for German recipes'.[11]

The summer of 1940 began to see increasing concern with the immobilisation of vehicles. Drivers were not allowed to leave them unattended during daylight hours unless they had taken away the ignition key or some vital part of the mechanism; in this way the enemy would be denied, it was hoped, a free ride. The police were empowered to immobilise vehicles themselves, if necessary. Of course, there were many exceptions, and exceptions to the exceptions, and very soon regulations were full of phrases like: 'it shall not be necessary to comply with the provisions of this paragraph save to the extent that, where the construction of the vehicle so permits, either of the requirements in sub-paragraph (a) of this paragraph shall be complied with'.[12] It is to be noticed that such regulations were examples of ministerial orders only, not of legislation. Covering enactments had been passed on the outbreak of war. There were so many more ways in which the citizen could fall foul of the law—especially if he owned a vehicle—and this is to say nothing of the body of restrictions covering blackout enforcement, curfews and increasing inhibition of movement.

Mr Pitcher still remembers his identity card number. As a child it was taken for granted by him that people carried this at all times as one was liable to be stopped in the street by police or troops for a check. It was not unusual for armed troops to scrutinise a complete busload of people. An area 20 miles inland from the coast was declared a defence zone. People from outside could not enter without special reasons and those inside had to obey restrictions on travel and they were certainly not allowed to carry a camera or field glasses. Rather alarmingly, car headlights had to be fitted with special shields which completely blocked out the bottom half of the beam. Meanwhile, the top half showed through three narrow slits covered by a hood. In this way, no light could be seen from the air. No lights were allowed inside a bus or train except for small blue-covered ones which were just good enough for people to find their seats.

Mrs Burgess seems to have quite enjoyed the pitch-darkness

involved in her Red Cross work and recalls how the masked torches looked like glow-worms. The town seemed cut off, like an island. People were not allowed to go onto the beach at Eastbourne and she herself never went up to London during the War. People felt less necessity to travel and did not feel like moving out if their family was in the town. They seemed to need the security of their familiar surroundings.[13] Major Batten found the prevailing air of secrecy rather oppressive. His Home Guard units were always being turned away from certain areas for no obvious reason. There were mysterious comings and goings of high-ranking officers and officials; and there were restrictions on talk. The *Grenadier,* often the focus of unofficial Home Guard activity, displayed notices such as 'Be like Dad. Keep Mum!' One night the Major was in there when somebody told him to come outside—there had been some loose talk going on. There were two women in the public bar and they had been talking about their Canadian boy friends going down to West Sussex. Just then a Canadian Army car drew up and two military police emerged and asked which bar the women were in. After a while the women were escorted out of the pub and 'given an awful wigging about their loose talk'.[14]

The newspapers began to report prosecutions for breaking regulations soon after the outbreak of war. A certain Lewes resident was fined £10 for taking photographs of ships in Newhaven Harbour. He pleaded ignorance of the Emergency Powers. He was not the only one to have had little idea of the changed circumstances. A man was summoned at Hailsham for camping within 10 miles of the coast.[15] Lt.Col. Gwynne, the Chairman of the Magistrates at the Hailsham Sessions, variously described as 'fearsome' and 'terrifying', seems to have had a fairly robust attitude towards Defence Regulations. In July 1941 he described them as an 'absolute farce'. It seems that there had been two cases of people entering defence areas without good reason. No steps, however, were taken to see that such people left the district. This, the Lieutenant-Colonel felt, was the Chief Constable's responsibility. He complained that examination points were often in the middle of an area instead of at its border. He was particularly exasperated by the case of a woman who had come from Ilford to Hellingly to visit the hospital. It seemed extraordinary, he felt, that people were unaware that a prohibited area was one which they were prevented from entering for holiday and pleasure.[16] The

Sussex Express itself weighed in with the suggestion that very few of the newspaper's own readers would be able to give an accurate account of the defence areas; and yet a Sussex magistrate was fining people because of their ignorance.[17]

Communications were restricted as well. The R.D.C., in the very first month of the war, found itself responsible for controlling the use of hooters, homing or racing pigeons, postcards to neutral countries, loose talk about B.B.C. transmitters, and reports of shipping. The cinema in Hailsham was closed down on September 8th, but re-opened on the 15th.[18] The ever-diminishing area of activity open to people was further emphasised when November 5th celebrations were abolished—a considerable blow to East Sussex where many villages have their own bonfire societies. Postal facilities were curtailed and there was to be only one delivery a day.[19]

The daily meat and drink of the Hailsham Petty Sessions was provided by the infringement of blackout regulations. Hailsham had blackout rehearsals in July and August 1939. This rather inconvenient exercise lasted from 12 midnight until 4 a.m. during which time 'no lights were to be visible from outside any building'.[20] The courts really started enforcing fines in January 1940 and several people were fined ten shillings for 'showing lights during the hours of darkness'. Fines were given for showing too much light from cars and also for neglecting to paint their bumpers and running boards white.[21] During August Lieutenant-Colonel Gwynne heard several cases connected with lights and admonished the public because the Air force had reported the whole Hailsham area to be a blaze of lights at night. There were 20 cases in one September session and people were being fined up to £20 and being threatened with prison. This Draconian treatment is clearly connected with the increasing tempo of air-raid warnings and the first cases of people being out after curfew were heard at this time. The usual defence was ignorance of the regulations. By the start of October, prison sentences were being given out for lighting offences.[22]

Hailsham was the centre of a rural area and regulations concerning agriculture impinged heavily upon the farming community. The Ministry of Agriculture had very clear ideas about what should be grown and enforced these through local War Agricultural Committees. The County Committee set targets which the local committees were expected to reach. These local committees coincided with the Rural Districts and that at Hailsham usually met at the *Grenadier*—although the very first meeting was at Deudneys Farm, Herstmonceux. These men were appointed by the County and were themselves working farmers, serving in a voluntary capacity. As usual, they were able to bend the rules for local circumstances—especially as some of the quotas were incapable of being realised due to lack of machinery. The Committee could make very detailed orders about which crops to grow—cereals were especially favoured. They rationed fertilizers and dairy cake. They could also issue ploughing orders. Persuasion was tried at first, but compulsion was in the background.[23] At the very beginning of the War it was stated that 20,000 acres of grassland were to be ploughed up in East Sussex in order to save the strain of importing grain and a careful eye was kept on the collection and distribution of fat stock for slaughter—Hailsham was an important collecting centre in this respect.[24]

Mr Salvage worked at Knight's Nurseries which switched from its usual output of garden plants to intensive food production on the outbreak of war. This was on the orders of the War Agricultural Committee. He feels that this committee contained some 'peculiar types'. One inspector tried to prevent them growing tarragon seed for Carters when, it seems, he was unable to distinguish these seeds from those meant for flower beds.[25] Major Batten had considerably less patience with the 'War Ag'. He clearly resented being told which fields to plough up and which to reserve for cattle. One official was told that it was impossible to graze a certain field because it had been overgrazed for the last sixty years and was probably disease-ridden. Having sold the cattle, he couldn't afford to re-stock anyway, in spite of what the Committee wanted. For refusing to obey this order he was called to Lewes where he expressed himself forcefully to the tribunal there. They threatened him with retribution for 'spreading alarm and despondence'. The result was that he was unable to renew the lease on the farm.[26]

The B.B.C. had been restricted to a single service and there was no local radio at the time. Local newspapers, from the summer of 1940 onwards, were being less specific about the facts, restricting themselves to warnings about being a chatterbox and gossiping. A man was fined at Hailsham for spreading rumours during July.[27]

The R.D.C., apart from concerning itself with the removal of name signs, was intrigued with the appearance of 'offensive propaganda' on bridges and walls. Reports were coming in of 'strange signs' made on pavements, possibly, it was felt, the work of schoolchildren. All this was slightly disturbing.[28] Hard information needed to be clearly conveyed if rumours were not to take over. The Ministry of Information sought the co-operation of local authorities in the spreading of news, especially 'in the event of there being a crisis so acute as to suspend the normal means of communication'.[29] Miss Knowles found that this involved her as an A.R.P. worker. The Ministry of Defence supplied Hailsham Civil Defence with three loudspeaker vans. These were rather elderly and had to be occasionally 'exercised', so that they would be able to start in the event of an emergency. There were times when she had to tour the district and broadcast information. She remembers that after about a hundred repetitions of the same paragraph it became a little boring. She adds, rather wistfully, that she wasn't really allowed to add elements of light relief. These cars had more or less unlimited supplies of petrol and their tanks had to be kept full. Consequently, all sorts of requirements were made of them. Various V.I.P.'s and mysterious personages had to be driven to secret destinations, for instance. At one stage, the vans were involved in the delivery of pies. A survey of various factories was made to find out if they would like these to supplement their rations. They were delivered twice weekly, but the experiment did not last long, probably because of the quality of the pies.[30]

Meanwhile, much of Hailsham's life continued in its time-honoured way. The pavilion cinema probably had its finest hour during the years of the War and there were even demands to have it open on Sundays—this from 'a competent military authority'.[31] In 'a certain Sussex town' the Vicar asked a lady of the parish to give a performance with her young girl dancers. He was persuaded to waive the admission charges, perhaps because of entertainment tax; voluntary offerings would be acceptable. It was protested that this might encourage young children to flood what was meant to be a very serious show and as a result placards appeared announcing in large type 'No children under 16 admitted'. This resulted, of course, in the hall being crowded to capacity by patrons seeking 'adult entertainment'.[32] The Hailsham Cricket Club carried on, albeit in an attenuated fashion, throughout 1940 and the Evening W.I.

which had ceased to meet at the outbreak of war, resumed in the *Grenadier* during April 1940.[33] The town still had an appearance of normality and the everyday appearance of the town's war effort will be considered further in the next chapter.

CHAPTER SIX

A Time to Knit

The town contained a series of overlapping structures concerned with what might be called the non-violent war effort, a world away from guns and bombs. The structures pre-dated the War and were quite happy to adapt to the new circumstances.

The Women's Institute was one such organisation. At the request of the Ministry of Agriculture, the W.I. became the focus for food preservation. Depots for bottling, canning and jam-making were set up at various points in the County and any village, through its W.I., could obtain sugar for jam-preservation. There were 135 W.I's in the County at the outbreak of war and most of them were involved in this sort of activity.[1] The records of the Hailsham W.I. are full of the politics of jam-making. This, of course, needed sugar additional to normal rations and the local secretary had to approach the Food Committee for permits. Priority was given to rhubarb and blackberries. Permits were obtained and the extra rations ready by May 1940. By 1941 the East Sussex Federation was clearly bringing pressure to bear on the Hailsham ladies to extend their jam-making horizons and there was talk of a Centre in Hailsham itself. Eventually this scheme was rejected but it was agreed to write to Messrs Newberry of Battle to see if a scheme could be arranged with them to purchase surplus fruit. By July 1941 we find that a Fruit Preservation Centre was already in operation at Magham Down.[2]

Meanwhile, and not at all surprisingly, controversy over jam-making had reached scandalous proportions. It was threatening to oust the war itself as a topic of discussion. The whole scheme was criticised as 'quite mad' by no less a person than Lt. Col. Gwynne. There was considerable difficulty in getting the ladies to work it properly. They were supposed to lend their pots and pans to the Centres—but wartime shortages were restricting their enthusiasm to do so. The Centres were only allowed to pay wholesale prices for fruit. Thus, a producer could get 5d. for a pound of gooseberries privately, but only 3d. at a Centre. Apparently, experts were being paid £5 a week to go round inspecting the jam-making methods whilst busy and experienced members of the W.I. were expected to travel some distance to a Centre instead of making jam at home. The controversy raged on during July 1941. All of people's pent-up impatience with bureaucracy and regulations seemed to vent itself on the jam-making scheme. The Sussex Express quite openly stated that the public was now so hedged in by restrictions that there was considerable confusion, especially as people were unused to regimentation. Apparently, only surplus fruit was supposed to be taken to the Centres. The Ministry of Food expected growers to bottle and sell all of the fruit they could. Owing to the shortage of sugar, the government encouraged the setting up of Centres to prevent wastage. The main problem with selling surplus fruit was the difficulty in obtaining transport for such small quantities. Questions, it seems, were asked in Parliament.[3]

W.I. members were deluged with advice on recipes. Potato recipe books were given out to members and Miss Knowles, already mentioned in connection with her Civil Defence work, demonstrated how to operate an outdoor cooking fire in an emergency. However, much W.I. activity was directed towards the general area of 'comforts for the troops'. Such was the enthusiasm for knitting that permission was given for the needles to click away even during lectures. Money was raised through Mrs Moon's 'White Elephant' window in her shop at the corner of Battle Road for the War Fund and had brought in £60 by February 1941. Felt slippers were needed in the hospital for evacuee children and a lady offered her own home and her expertise for classes in how to make these from old felt hats. A great deal of the knitting went to hospitalised servicemen via the Red Cross and the value of this was recognised by making it possible for members of the W.I. to obtain wool free of coupons through the W.V.S. offices. There were competitions of all sorts in connection with wool—one, for instance, 'for the best baby garment made from non-coupon wool'.[4] The Parish Magazine was also much concerned with knitting. In 1939 capable knitters were encouraged to collect wool from the W.V.S. at the Midland Bank Chambers. The area W.V.S. had a target of a thousand balaclava helmets and Hailsham had provided 20 of these by January 1940, as well as six scarves, sea-boot stockings and a body belt. There was a sewing and knitting depot at the 'Old Forge', Magham Down and an increasing amount of knitted articles flowed through it from knitted shirts to hot water bottle covers. On a national level, the depot for knitted garments for the Royal Navy was able to process half a million garments and seems to have supplied half the fleet.[5]

Knitting did not exhaust the resources of the W.I. as far as the Armed Services were concerned. Books were collected for the Navy and a fund was set up to replace the Royal Sussex Regiment's brass instruments which had been lost during action. Gramophone records as well as fruit and flowers were collected for Hellingly Military Hospital and several ladies volunteered to let members of the forces have baths once a week in their own homes. Members were encouraged to entertain lonely soldiers.[6] Several members of the W.I. were also members of the W.V.S. and it is worth pointing out that these organisations became a clearing-house for a great variety of wartime activities, from propaganda about salvage to assistance in Civil Defence work. One of the functions of the W.V.S. was to service canteens for troops and evacuees. Mr Pitcher, who worked as a baker's roundsman at the time, used to serve the canteen with large four pound sandwich loaves.[7] Mrs Hanks worked at the hall 'next to the Court House'. It was open from morning to night and she used to cook for the troops—eggs, bacon and beans on toast. A huge summerhouse had been put up at the back of the hall and this was converted into a bathroom for the troops with hot and cold water. There were so many wanting baths that the customers were issued with numbers so that they could be kept in rotation.[8] The W.V.S. organised the Blood Transfusion Service[9] and were clearly in a privileged position. They feature strongly in the minutes of the R.D.C. and its various committees. Mrs Gardner was the W.V.S. District Organiser and she clearly carried weight with the local authority. They were heavily involved in the complex evacuation and energetic in the collection and storage of salvage.[10] The W.V.S. also ran the Rest Centres for victims of bombing and asked the W.I. to supply games and packs of cards for use there.[11]

The Parish Church was another of the group of interlocking organisations involved in Wartime activities and the Parish Magazine features many of the names prominent in the W.I. and the W.V.S. The Vicar's newsletter, written by the Rev. Macklin C.

Chapman, M.A., expresses concerns beyond the merely parochial. A reference to the Church Mission to Jews in September shows an awareness of the sufferings of European Jewry. He had, apparently, met some of the refugees and had been considerably shocked by some of the stories they had to tell. Actual church services were affected to the extent that lighting restrictions curtailed Evensong during the winter months. Church unity seems to have been encouraged insofar as clergymen of the various denominations in the town held united prayer meetings 'on behalf of the fighting forces and national unity'. The Sunday schools recognised the gravity of the situation by deciding to cancel prizes 'until happier times'. It was hoped, however, that this would not encourage children to be slack in their attendance. As with other publications, the tone tends to become markedly serious during the summer of 1940. The King, writes the Vicar, called for a national day of prayer on September 8th and there was concern about how to treat an air-raid warning should it occur during a service. It was pointed out that there was a public shelter in Vicarage Field but that any wishing to remain in church should move to the centre of the nave to avoid flying splinters. Hailsham servicemen, especially if they were missing, were prayed for, and there was considerable rejoicing when two of these emerged as prisoners of war. The bombs which dropped on Hailsham in August 1940 led Searle's to advertise in the Parish Magazine. They were offering anti-splinter nets at a shilling and three farthings as well as some paper blinds and blackout curtains. The latter varied in price from 2/6d to 2/11d per yard.[12]

Mr Pitcher can remember witnessing the removal of various iron gates and railings from buildings in Hailsham. These were to be taken away and used in the munitions factories. No compensation was paid but the amputated stubs of railings in various parts of the town, including the front of Cortlandt, bear witness to this assault on Victorian ironwork.[13] Scrap metal dumps were organised in every parish covered by the R.D.C.[14] and throughout the country as a whole, the scrap metal drive is estimated to have produced half a million tons.[15] In July 1940 there was a drive by the R.D.C. for brass, silver, chrome, aluminium and steel. Again, the W.V.S. was the main agent in this sort of task and Ripley's yard was an important collecting centre.[16] Because of the drastic rationings in the town newsagents were unwilling to stock more newspapers than they were certain to sell. In May 1940 the Sussex Express offered cash by weight for old newspapers delivered to its offices.[17] The Hailsham R.D.C. had its own Salvage Committee and here again the emphasis was on waste paper. Collection was organised in conjunction with the normal bin-emptying and considerable efforts were made to save paper in the Council's own office work. It was suggested that the smallest size and thinnest quality should be used, typing should be single-spaced and both sides of paper should be used in writing letters. Old envelopes and scrap paper would have to do for calculations.[18]

It is difficult to avoid the impression that the *real* invasion of East Sussex was carried out not by the German armoured divisions but by the bomb-threatened evacuees of London. Hailsham prepared for the onslaught in something of a siege mentality long before the concept of a 'Nodal Point' had been seriously considered.

On 8th March 1939 the R.D.C. formed its Evacuation Committee. This faced the rather daunting prospect of 11,000 newcomers to the area, of whom half would be schoolchildren and their teachers and the other half would be children under school age and their mothers. Mr H.R. Maryan found himself the Parish Billeting Officer. By the beginning of May, forms for the reception of evacuees in billets had been received, rations of food to be issued at railheads had been planned, and detailed traffic schedules had been drawn up. Orders for blankets were being placed. At this time the term 'refugee' was in use—'evacuee' did not come into currency until the newcomers actually arrived.

At the beginning of September, 2,756 unaccompanied children and 1,931 children with mothers and teachers were unloaded at Polegate Station. Colonel Johnson personally took charge of this operation. They had to be processed through the Receiving Centres at the Social Hall, Corn Exchange, Victoria Hall and the Baptist school room. Within a day, 650 of these had been found homes in Hailsham and Magham Down. As usual, the W.V.S. was prominent in dealing with the influx.[19]

How did the newcomers and the entrenched residents strike each other? A certain Hailsham housewife states that 'the feeling of strangeness was mutual'.[20] One family seems to have had mixed feelings:

> A mother and two toddlers came; we tried to be helpful, but I cannot really say that they settled down happily. Their way of

life was as alien to us as ours was to them and, horror of horrors, they used only tinned milk.

However, this family was fortunate. Firstly, it was sunny weather and the children were able to spend most of their time outside; and secondly, it was not very long before the mother turned up one evening to say that she had decided to take the children back to London.[21]

Mrs Mobbs moved down to Hailsham with sixty children from London's dockland. Some were as young as three and many were with their mothers. She recalls that it was strange at first to be away from London with its bustling life. The train was packed with children, each carrying a suitcase and gas mask. They had never heard of Polegate, of course, but there were coaches there waiting to take them on to Hailsham. They appreciated the ladies of the W.V.S. who helped to ameliorate this awkward transition. The children were agog at the unfamiliar and rather forbidding open countryside during the ride to Hailsham. They were whisked into the Corn Exchange at the back of 'The Crown'. They realised that this was in what Hailsham called its 'High Street'—but it was difficult to understand why there were so few shops in it and why it was so quiet. Very soon the children and teachers were allocated to billets. Mrs Mobbs found herself in rooms over one of the shops in the High Street. She and her own family felt strange at first and found it difficult to fit into their new way of life. She recalls the severe shortage of water in the hot September weather. They were allowed one bucket of water a day in which to wash, clean the floor, cook, and wash clothes. They had to pour it down the toilet in order to flush it. Mrs Mobb's children were given the use of a hall under the Congregational Church as a schoolroom. They were in business. There were some initial difficulties with the Catholic priest, about the teaching of religion to the Catholic children, but this was soon overcome. They became the best of friends. In fact, Mrs Mobbs found the reception of the evacuees very positive. Baker's, the clothing shop, gave all London children a 10 per cent discount. They appreciated the projects laid on by organisations like the W.I. and their gifts of toys, games and puzzles. She organised concerts by the children themselves to which the host families were invited. Sister Blackbourne, the District Nurse, was seen as a helpful friend, as was Mr Hanks, the Sussex Express reporter. Some of the children were billeted at Michelham Priory and Mrs Mobbs remembers her anxiety about the children running wild in the Tudor halls.[22]

October 1939 saw a spate of 'evacuee' stories in the local press. Sussex, of course, has had a tradition of isolation in spite of its nearness to London. However, the stories betray some degree of social pre-supposition and their main value lies in the assumptions of the writers rather than in their precise truth. One suspects that some must be slightly apocryphal:

> One small boy was going home on a train this week and was discussing his experiences in Sussex. In tones that showed me he was deeply impressed he confided:— 'I learnt to say "pardon", I did. You have to speak so posh here'.
>
> A little evacuee wrote from a farm in the country: 'do come down and see me Mummy, but do bring your gas mask because the pigs smell'.
>
> Scene: middle class house. Evacuee children getting down to dinner with good appetites. Lady of the house: 'I don't know how on earth I'm going to feed you children on 8s.6d a week'. Small boy (being helpful): 'you will have to go out to work like mummy does'.
>
> A cottager led two little boys to a nicely laid table on which there was a dish of stewed steak, potatoes etc. and they said, 'that ain't the kind of dinner we have'. The good woman, fearing it was not good enough, asked, 'What sort of dinner do you usually have?'. She received the answer, 'A pint of beer and a hunk of bread and cheese'.
>
> Another hostess took her little charges upstairs and showed them their beds. They stared at the snowy whiteness and said that they had never slept in that sort of thing. 'Where do you sleep then?' she asked. 'In a box with straw in it', they answered, 'same as the dog'.
>
> There was another big surprise for the householder who found that the husband of the young woman billeted on her had arrived and, without asking permission, had made himself a bed in her bath.[23]

However, there are some hard facts which give one pause to think. The Billeting Tribunal, which had the power to remove evacuees if a good enough reason could be found, heard a request for the removal of two small boys, who, it was alleged, never laughed or smiled. Another woman from London complained that the woman she was billeted on obviously didn't want her and expected the evacuees to leave the house whenever she herself did. In this case, permission was granted.[24] The Hailsham Evacuation Committee soon had its fair share of complaints. There were head lice, for example. However, the London County Council soon provided an auxiliary for the cleansing of dirty heads. The Council was concerned with the relieving of householders 'of the unreasonable burden placed upon billeting of dirty and undisciplined evacuees'. Arrangements were made for the provision of hostel accommodation to deal with such cases. This was at Spring Lodge. As a consequence, the Medical Officer of Health pointed out that genuinely ill children were being denied admission so that 'dirty or undisciplined children could be kept away from their billets as long as possible'. He said that the hospitals 'were never intended to be used as dumps for undesirable children'. A Mr F. complained that he and his daughter had contracted impetigo from an evacuee billeted on them: was he expected to pay his own doctor's bill?'[25]

Mr Maryan, the Parish Billeting Officer, remembers that a great deal of trouble arose from billeting mothers with children. On his own initiative and without the backing of the Council, he took over four or five houses. A cash receipt surviving from September 1939 shows that certain people were setting a good example in billeting. Mr Maryan himself had two boys whom he found 'clean but not very truthful'. He grew quite fond of them but they never really settled down to life in a small town. The District Billeting Officer, Sir James Sifton, was looking after a Mrs Beeton and her three children, whilst the Vicar was responsible for a certain Frank and John Cuthbert.[26] The rate set at the start of the War for billeting was ten shillings and sixpence for the first child and two shillings less for the others. This was supposed to cover full board and lodging. By February 1940, however, food prices had risen by 14 per cent and people were beginning to lose money on the transaction.[27] Mr Maryan's position put him at the receiving end of most of the complaints. One householder said that his evacuees were not quite clear about the use of toilets and water kept on coming through the ceiling. Some of the boys wet the bed and on one occasion Mr Maryan had a mattress thrown out of the window at him. The most persistent matter, however, was head lice, especially with the longer-haired girls. The hosts thought that they were dealing with the problem by washing the childrens' hair, but this only made things worse. The County Medical Officer of Health eventually brought down a woman from London who dealt with the problem by rubbing in oil and scratching the creatures out. On one occasion Mr Maryan received a phone call from a woman announcing that she was going to murder the mother of one of the evacuees billeted on her. It seems that a triangular situation was developing between the two women and one man in the household. Nothing was done about this and the murder failed to materialise: 'they merely pulled each other's hair out'.[28]

There was a whole group from the Rotherhithe Nautical School, under their teacher Mr Stead, who took over the large house on the corner of London Road and Summerheath Road. Some of them decided to start walking home now and again and it would be Mr Stead's task to follow them up the A22 in his car. Usually he made them walk back instead of giving them a lift. Many of these boys ended up at Battle Road School and quite a few of these were admitted by the time school opened on 18th September 1939—late because of the War situation. The evacuee children who spent time at the school were mainly from London although there was a sprinkling from the Portsmouth area. Of the Londoners, only a minority came from the inner city—Rotherhithe, Bermondsey and the like—the rest came from outer suburbs such as Brixton and Norwood, some from as far out as Croydon or Wimbledon. About half of them were accompanied by mothers or other female relatives—never by fathers. They seem to have been billeted fairly evenly around the town, but a quarter found homes in the surrounding villages of the school catchment area. By Christmas, half the evacuee children in the school had returned home and very few remained by the early summer of 1940. A few more children arrived from London when the school opened in September 1940 but they were far outnumbered by children coming in from bomb-threatened Eastbourne at this time—20 in all.[29]

During the spring of 1940 there was considerable apprehension as plans leaked out for the billeting of another 1100 children in the area. However, this fear never materialised. As the prospect of invasion began to become imminent the tide began to turn the other way. Plans were made for evacuation from the East Sussex area. Most of the original newcomers to the area were re-evacuated to South Wales by the middle of July 1940. Most of the hostels and some hospitals were released from requisition, staff had their engagements terminated and bedding and furniture were put into store. However, this state of affairs did not continue for long. The start of September saw another turn of the screw when people in the Pevensey area found themselves living in a prohibited zone and encouraged to move inland. Also, evacuees were coming in from coastal towns like Eastbourne. The R.D.C. requisitioned empty houses for families but accommodation was difficult to find. On November 4th the Ministry of Health asked the Council to be ready to accommodate 100 hop pickers but fortunately only 30 arrived.[30]

At the beginning of January 1941 there were 1500 evacuees from coastal towns in the area and by spring many of the Parish Billeting Officers had resigned, giving various reasons. One gets the feeling that they were exhausted by this long period of work on a thankless task. However, Miss M.M. Hampton, the Chairman of the Evacuation Committee, and Sir James Sifton stuck to their posts throughout the whole period. Really, one can only wonder at their endurance.[31]

While one set of R.D.C. Committees had been concerned with Civil Defence and another had busied itself with plans for an invasion, another one, the Evacuation Committee, dealt with what the town perceived as a genuine occupation. People reacted to the influx from London as a foreign intrusion into the life of the market town on the level of actual alien forces. Reactions, of course, varied with individual temperament but both sides seem to have been happy to shrug off this episode in their lives and return to normal.

CHAPTER SEVEN
Forty Years On

German propaganda of the early war period represents England as a dull, listless society. Most of the sources we have studied do not give this impression. The immediate impression is one of energy and commitment. What is particularly impressive is the dull routine work carried out by large numbers of volunteers. A pertinent example is the Civil Defence tasks carried out during the winter of 1939-40 when men were asked to have showers with no towels. The Decontamination Parties and Searchlight Crews on the marshes plaintively asked for radios to while away the endless hours of waiting for the emergency which never came. Captain Baker recorded, without any particular sense of heroism, 'that I really ought to do something'. Mr Salvage got on quite unthinkingly with the rather unglamorous work of an A.R.P. warden. Even before the war there were committed people, such as Mr Pitcher's parents, who did the necessary preliminary work of gas mask distribution. It is certainly possible to admire the publican who spent much of the War preparing for his role as a spy if the Germans landed and did so at the cost of a certain loss of respect among the villagers who thought that he was a shirker for not joining the Home Guard.

Forty years later, most of us who have had an easeful life can only wonder how all this dedication managed to survive one outstanding fact; that in reality, the crisis never came to areas like ours. Compared to London, or even to Eastbourne, the effects of war on Hailsham were distinctly limited. The huge Civil Defence organisation simply had to watch and wait. In comparison to what had been anticipated, the actual incidents were very occasional. The Home Guard never had to face an actual enemy and it must have become increasingly clear after the 'invasion summer' of 1940 that such an event was not going to happen. The desperate structuring of Hailsham's resources against invasion had to be maintained: serious meetings had to take place and reports needed to be prepared. And yet, the whole affair must have become increasingly fictional in the minds of officials 'in the know'. The temptation to become casual must have been strong. Sometimes the sources give hints of this. For example, the growing incidence of blackout prosecutions represents either an increasing element of carelessness on the part of the public or increased enthusiasm for enforcement by the authorities. The continuous appeals, through the Parish Magazine, for more Civil Defence workers suggest that there were certain areas of apathy in the town. The records, of course, tend to reflect mainly the activities of the committed.

At the intimate level of history we find useful correctives to more general accounts of the past. We can counterpoint the German invasion of Russia in the summer of 1941 with what people in Hailsham were talking about—the intricacies of fruit-preservation. The first year of the war has as much to tell us about the town's response to evacuation from this point of view as it does about geopolitics. However, the study of intimate history at a relatively recent period has its own problems. The war years, in particular, are part of our national consciousness and very dear in memory to the people who took part in it. Their sense of achievement and pride in having 'pulled through' can overcast the memory. Some quotations from our informants will put our problems into focus:

> Everybody seemed to be free from bitchiness and backbiting.
>
> The whole war was a time of solidarity; everybody I encountered was behind every effort you were making.
>
> People were marvellous at that time; they never complained; everyone was willing to help everyone else—unlike now.
>
> There was a deep national feeling and petty differences disappeared.

Other informants have a more rueful tone and emphasise the lack of cheese or the way that they missed onions. Some informants are quite guarded in their approach. Captain Baker, describing the Home Guard, felt that his account of their activities might make it all sound rather farcical:

> ... but in the mood of the time, with invasion probable, so far as we knew, at any moment, we were deadly serious

and anything ... we could do to resist was like gold dust. It is impossible to say how people would have reacted but the general feeling was such at the time that I doubt if the Germans would have had it easy'.[1]

Much seems to depend on the character and temperament of the witnesses and participants. Major Batten seems to display the Wealden farmer's typically robust attitude towards authority. His condemnations of what he saw as the silliness of certain Home Guard activities and his firm stand against pressures from the War Ag. Committee suggest a natural reaction against bureaucracy. One feels that he sometimes felt impatient over the obsession with secrecy; this in spite of a manifestly deep commitment to defending the country. In general, Major Batten's tone is highly realistic: he, for instance, saw the Home Guard's role as rather suicidal—and this was not just in hindsight. The detailed diary he kept throughout the whole period confirms this.[2] Sometimes, people's perceptions are downright contradictory. Mr Salvage found nothing but co-operation from householders in his sector on the matter of blackout. Mr F. Clark, on the other hand, had a different experience as a warden:

> Some people were very shirty about putting their lights out. They didn't take any notice at all—didn't think it was worth it. I used to go in and tell them off, saying, 'if you don't do it, I'll do it for you'. So I went in and turned the lights off myself.

So where do we find the truth here? Are the two wardens talking about different periods in the War? Did their approaches to people evoke different responses?[3]

The identification of precise facts can cause problems. This is especially true of bomb and aircraft stories. People's memories can foreshorten, and separate incidents can be confused or telescoped together. The stick of bombs falling on Hailsham in August 1940 is recounted in a variety of ways. At least once, it is confused with the bouncing bomb of 1943. The incident when the Hurricane rammed an enemy fighter is difficult to disentangle through purely oral testimony. Eye witness accounts are invaluable for lively detail—diving under the kitchen table; coal falling out of the sky like confetti; and the fact that hitherto uncommunicative neighbours spoke to each other for the first time in Ersham Road after the bomb fell—all this adds to our knowledge. However, we have been thankful for the precise, if laconic, accounts registered in the Civil Defence Incident Books. It is hard, sometimes, to identify people. There was a sense of relief when Mr Roberts was able to recognise himself standing by the 'Molotov Slinger' shown on the cover page. In fact, photographs are particularly useful in this sort of study. Mrs Mobbs with her evacuees takes us back with a jolt to the appearance of wartime children. Mrs Burgess was able to identify at least half a dozen Civil Defence workers from a fading print to jog her memory.

In a more serious respect, the roles of various people can be difficult to untangle. Many of the participants tended to be the type of energetic individual who was involved in a variety of jobs. Mrs Hanks belonged the W.V.S. and took part in firewatching. She made camouflage nets and became heavily involved in the evacuation scheme. Apart from this, she spent time helping her husband in his reporting for the Sussex Express. Miss Knowles worked for the A.R.P. during the daytime, driving vehicles and helping to produce the H.A.R.P. magazine as well as taking her turn on night duty in the Control Room. She ferried a mobile kitchen around the countryside and found time during the evening to act as Commandant of the Girls' Training Corps. Some of the organisations themselves had overlapping functions and membership. A great deal of the information relating to the W.I., W.V.S., Red Cross and St John's Ambulance overlaps and it is almost as if belonging to one were tantamount to belonging to all. It is a relief to find, however, that people rarely seemed to belong to both the Home Guard and the A.R.P. There is also considerable difficulty in sorting out the multiplicity of Rest Centres and canteens in the town.

The group made some effort, discreetly, to discover the more unsavoury side of wartime Hailsham. Was there a black market, for instance? Informants who worked in the Food Office specifically deny this and the court records seem strangely silent. Most of the trouble here seemed to concern infringements of blackout regulations. There must have been some excitement concerning relationships between ladies in Hailsham and locally-stationed troops. It could hardly have been quite so bland as the W.I. minutes seem to suggest. Again, people seem to remember nothing about this. How much apathy was there really? There are hints in the R.D.C. minutes of difficulties in recruitment to the various Civil Defence organisations and there are the mysterious slogans chalked on walls hinting at 'offensive propaganda'. The Sussex County Magazine contains comments directed at 'do-nothings'—This means those who, when there are a multitude of war jobs to do, spend their time standing at the kerb with their hands in their pockets gazing vacantly at the passing traffic.

The sources seem reliable enough. What can distort the truth is our own selection from the sources. Members of our own group are just as capable as anyone else of selecting material which supports what they expect to find in the first place. It is also possible that members of groups like ours do not move in the sort of circles in which information about the black market and suchlike is easily available. Our informants themselves are also subject to selective memory—the high points are often remembered best. What seemed commonplace at the time might be thoroughly interesting to us 40 years later. It seems certain that what newspapers reported in wartime was perfectly correct but highly selective. Wartime secrecy can still have an effect. There is information connected with the 'British Resistance' which people are still unwilling to divulge and certain facts about the bombing of the Radar station on the Pevensey Marshes simply do not add up. The Incident Book states quite clearly that there were casualties and yet two members of the Rescue Services called in from Hailsham quite independently deny this. Was the whole installation so secret that even the A.R.P. could not be trusted?

Certain wartime events are etched sharply into people's memories. Mrs Burgess remembers the announcement of the actual outbreak of the War, turning to her husband and declaring that it was the end of their sort of world. Again something cataclysmic was expected. However, she herself has no recollection of feeling bored with the War at any stage. Like others, she recalls the positive aspects and certain feelings of spontaneity, Members of the Red Cross would quite freely walk up to soldiers in the street and ask them to go for dances.[4] A Hailsham housewife remembers sharing a huge hunk of cheese with a group of servicemen who were perfect strangers to her.[5] Mrs White recalls cycling into Hailsham, tin hat on her service strap and gas mask on her back; she was on her way to First Aid duty and would share the upstairs room of Dr Shaw's house with other volunteers. One of her vivid memories is of incendiaries over the marsh. They went up onto the balcony, 'and I can only liken the scene to a spread-out bonfire night procession of flaming torches flickering in the blackness, and somewhere in the midst a larger conflagration'. Her group was called out to the scene of the bombing at Rushlake Green in November 1940 when people were killed in a bus. Their unit vehicle left the road and fell into a ditch. They scrambled out unhurt but had to take refuge in the ditch with enemy bombers overhead. They were unable to go any further and had to be ferried back to Hailsham, leaving the vehicle behind to be towed back the next day. Events like this might have been alarming at the time but give a heightened perspective of life in recollection.[6] Miss Knowles clearly enjoyed the all-night sessions in the Control Room and driving about the countryside in Ministry cars. Normal rules could be broken: respectable unescorted women did not enter pubs—but they could if they wore tin hats and they were on A.R.P. business. Members of the Home Guard spent nights in the churchyard. The rules were all topsy-turvy and there was not really *too* great danger. Best of all, people knew they were doing something obviously useful.

How were attitudes towards the War generated? There was radio and press, of course. At a local level they were mediated through organisations like the W.I. and the Parish Magazine which reached certain sections, at least, of the public. The Sussex Express reached a far wider public but was less cosy in its approach. As we have seen, there was criticism over the jam-making fiasco and the muddle over prohibited areas. The Sussex County Magazine went so far as to question the legitimacy of wartime telephone tapping, especially when it was used for such trivial offences as infringements of the food regulations.[7] However, the local publications never contain comments which might undermine basic war aims. Mr Hanks, the Sussex Express reporter for the Hailsham area, took part in the information process. Noted for his immaculate shorthand and accurate reporting, Each village in the Rural District was visited at the same time each week and we have him to thank for the snippets of press information scattered throughout this study.[8]

Surprisingly, there is not as much outright jingoism as we might imagine in the newspapers. There was, of course, the rejection of 'Appelkraut' a growing tendency to gloat over bombers shot down during 'murder raids'. A poem published in November 1940 has a certain rough-hewn quality which puts dark thoughts into the head of an imaginary ex-Lewes Bonfire boy turned pilot:

> It thrills your blood and makes you feel
> You really are alive,
> When pouring volleys into them
> They make a bad nose-dive.
>
> Or perhaps the very best of all
> Is when their oil tanks burn,
> And light us on our homeward way
> For miles on our return.[9]

An ex-member of the Hailsham Young People's Fellowship heard of the destruction of the church windows whilst serving in the forces.

> ... Those grandly glowing panes for ever gone,
> Spoiled by the desecrator's ruthless might;
> Those lovelier links with happier yesterday
> For ever blotted from our saddened sight.
> 'Sic transit gloria mundi'. Nought remains
> But splintered glass and twisted strips of lead ...[10]

NOTES AND REFERENCES

Chapter 1
1. *Sussex County Magazine*, March 1940.
2. All material subsequent to Note 1 is based on *Kelly's Sussex Directory*, 1938.

Chapter 2
1. Circular from the Commander of 'C' sub-area to police, local authorities, military units and LDV, 16.7.40, ESRO, CD Box 16.
2. German High Command instruction for Operation Sea Lion and appendices 30.8.40: translated in *Operation Sealion*, Ronald Wheatly, O.U.P. 1968.
3. Circular from Commander of 'C' sub-area to police, local authorities, military units and LDV, 16.7.40, ESRO, CD Box 16.
4. 'The Defence of the United Kingdom', Basil Collier, in *The Official History of the Second World War*, HMSO 1957.
5. Military appreciation of plans for casualties, 'C' sub-area by the Lt. Col. I/C 190 Field Ambulance, summer 1940, ESRO, CD Box.
6. Personal interview with Mr R. Dodds, wartime member of the Royal Sussex Regiment.
7. Written memories of Mr E. Pitcher.
8. Personal interview with Mr H. Maryan, wartime member of the Home Guard.
9. *The Home Guard can Fight*, HMSO 1940. A summary of lectures at the Osterley Park training school for Home Guards.
10. *The People's War*, Angus Calder, Panther, 1979.
11. *BLAST Magazine*, newsletter of 20th Sussex Battalion HG, undated.
12. Personal interview with Mr H. Maryan, wartime member of Hailsham HG.
13. Written memories of Captain R. Baker, wartime member of Hailsham HG.
14. Personal interviews with Mr J. Roberts, and with major O.A. Batten, both wartime members of Hailsham HG.
15. Nominal Role of 20th Sussex (Hailsham) Battalion, from ESRC, CD Box, undated.
16. Personal interview with Miss N. Knowles, Hailsham ARP worker.
17. *Farewell of the 20th Sussex Battalion, Home Guard*, Lt. Col. F.G. Crompton, 1944.
18. *Ibid*.
19. Mr J. Roberts.
20. Major O.A. Batten.
21. Captain R. Baker.
22. Major O.A. Batten.
23. Captain R. Baker.
24. Elementary Drill Memory Card, O/C Reading OTC, Gale and Polden Ltd, Aldershot, 1939.
25. *Op.cit. The Home Guard can Fight*.
26. Captain R. Baker.
27. Major O.A. Batten.
28. *BLAST magazine* newsletter of 20th Sussex Battalion, 10.9.41.
29. 20th Sussex Battalion Home Guard 3rd Anniversary Celebrations Programme, 16.5.43.
30. Major O.A. Batten.
31. *Sunday Times* Colour Supplement article series, issued 1969.
32. *Op.cit., The Home Guard can Fight*.

33. Mr H. Maryan.
34. Major O.A. Batten.
35. Personal interview with a member of a wartime secret communications group who wishes to remain anonymous.
36. Circular from Commander of 'C' Sub-Area to police, local authorities, military units and LDV, 16.7.40, ESRO, CD Box 16.
37. *Ibid*, 22.7.40.
38. Personal interview with Mr D. White, wartime member of the Territorial Army Unit at Park House, Hellingly, and with Mr T. Henry Wilson, wartime surgeon and medical officer in RAMC.
39. Personal information from a Ward Sister at Hellingly Hospital.
40. HRDC Record of Deaths due to War Operations.
41. Mr E. Pitcher.
42. Personal interview with a Hailsham housewife.
43. *Sussex Life*, September 1975.
44. HRDC. Record of Deaths due to War Operations.
45. Mr E. Pitcher.
46. SCM, July 1941.
47. *Hurricane Special*, Maurice Allward, Jon. Allan Ltd, and personal communication with Mr I. Turner, retired director of Green Bros.
48. Detailed information on the Pevensey Radar Station from Mr M.G. Scroggie (personal interview) and from Daphne Carne, *The Eyes of the Few*, Macmillan, 1960.
49. SECH, May 1942.
50. ESCC, A.R.P. Incident Book, 1940.

Chapter 3

The speculations about Mr Carr's frame of mind are firmly rooted in the Civil Defence records at ESRO and Hailsham RDC correspondence listed below.

1. Notes for the Deputy Parish Sub-Controller and Food Controller Para 13, Circular issued by SERO: undated but probably mid-1941. ESRO.
2. Hailsham RDC ARP Committee, 23.8.39.
3. *Sussex Express and County Herald*, Hailsham Edition, 19.4.41.
4. Survey of Hailsham NP carried out by SERO, April 1941, ESRO, CD Box.
5. Summary of Hailsham NP facilities 19.2.41, ESRO, CD Box. Letter from ARP Sub-Controller, Hailsham (Mr Carr) to County ARP Controller, 14.1.41, ESRO, CD Box.
6. Letter from Brigadier of 'C' Sub Area to police, local authorities, military units and LDV, 16.7.40, ESRO, CD Box.
7. *Ibid*, 22.7.40.
8. 'Nodal Points': *General Operational and Information and Instructions for Civil Authorities*, (The South East Regional Office's 'Yellow Book'), prepared by L.B. Burrows, June 1941, (Para.1), ESRO, CD Box 9.
9. Survey of Heathfield NP by SERO, 19.4.41, ESRO, CD Box.
10. Personal interview with Major Batten, wartime member of Hailsham Home Guard.
12. General Survey of Hailsham NP carried out by SERO, probably June 1941, ESRO, CD Box 9.
13. Notes for the Deputy Parish Sub-Controller and Food Organiser, Para 10: circular issued by SERO, undated, but probably mid-1941, ESRO, CD Box.
14. Instructions to Police by SERO, 11.8.40, ESRO, CD Box.
15. *Ibid*.
16. *Op.cit*, L.B. Burrows.

17. Letter from Brigadier of 'C' Sub-Area to police, local authorities, military units and LDV, 16.7.40, ESRO, CD Box.
18. Circular from SERO to 'All Scheme-Making Authorities and all Chief Constables in the Area', 12.5.40, ESRO, CD Box.
19. *Sussex Express and County Herald*, Hailsham Edition, 6.10.39.
20. Letter from A. Carr to Mr Martin 14.1.41, ESRO, CD Box. The comments about Mr Carr's anxieties on the previous pages are based largely on this letter.
21. Hailsham RDC Minutes of various sub-committees, 1939-41.
22. Letter from Brigadier of 'C' Sub-Area to police, local authorities, military units and LDV, 16.7.40, ESRO, CD Box.
23. Personal interview with Major Batten, wartime member of Hailsham Home Guard.
24. Information from various Hailsham residents collected by Captain R. Baker.
25. Personal interview with Miss Rous.
26. Survey of Hailsham NP after meeting between Hailsham officials and Ministry of Health Representatives, 19.2.41, ESRO, CD Box 9.
27. Civil Defence Survey of Hailsham NP by SERO, 10.2.41, ESRO CD Box.
28. Letter from A. Carr to H. Martin, 15.8.41, ESRO, CD Box 9.
29. Survey of Hailsham by SERO, April 1942, ESRO, CD Box.
30. *Ibid.*
31. *Op.cit.* L.B. Burrows.
32. CD Survey of Gardner Street by SERO, undated, probably mid-1941, by SERO, ESRO, CD Box.
33. *Sussex Express and County Herald* 21.6.40.
34. Instructions to police by SERO, 11.8.40 and July 1942, SERO, CD Box.
35. *Ibid.*
36. Hailsham RDC Special Evacuation Committee minutes, July and September 1940.
37. Written memories of Mr E. Pitcher.
38. Commentary on 'Yellow Book' (see note 8), issued by SERO, 2.3.42, CD Box 9.
39. Personal interview with Miss Rous.
40. Military appreciation of plans for casualties, 'C' Sub-Area, by the Lt. Col. I/C 190 Field Ambulance, Summer 1940, ESRO CD Box.
41. Map and list of roads for military traffic and civilian crossing points prepared for SERO by Police Divisions, 13.5.40, ESRO, CD Box 9.
42. Letter from SERO to Mr Martin, 14.5.40, CD Box 9.
43. Map and list of roads for military traffic and civilian crossing points prepared for SERO by Police divisions, 13.5.40, ESRO, CD Box 9.
44. Instructions to police by SERO, 11.8.40 and July 1942, ESRO, CD Box.
45. *Ibid*, 11.8.40.
46. CD. Survey of Hailsham NP, 10.2.41, by SERO, ESRO, CD Box.
47. Written memories of Mrs D. White.
48. Instructions to police by SERO, 11.8.40, ESRO, CD Box.
49. CD. Survey of Hailsham NP by SERO, 10.2.41. ESRO, CD Box.
50. Survey of Hailsham NP after meeting between Hailsham officials and Ministry of Health representatives, 19.2.41, ESRO, CD Box 9.
51. Survey of Hailsham NP carried out by SERO, probably June 1941, ESRO CD Box 9.
52. SERO Architect's report on Hailsham NP 21.3.41, ESRO, CD Box.
53. Letter from A. Carr to H. Martin, 15.8.41, ESRO, CD Box.
54. SERO Survey of Hailsham NP, April 1942, ESRO, CD Box.

55. Survey of Hailsham NP carried out by SERO, probably June 1941, ESRO, CD Box.
56. *Ibid.*
57. Notes for the Deputy Parish Sub-Controller and Food Organiser, Para 13; circular issued by SERO, undated, but probably mid-1941. ESRO, CD Box.
58. Personal interview with Hailsham Food Executive Officer, Mr Faulkner.
59. *Ibid.*
60. Hailsham WI Minutes, August 1941.
61. Instructions to police by SERO, 11.8.40, ESRO, CD Box.
62. SERO Circular on Emergency Water Supply, Feb. 1942.
63. General Survey of Hailsham NP by SERO, probably June 1941, ESRO, CD Box 9.
64. *Ibid.*

Chapter 4

1. *Front Line*, HMSO, 1945.
2. Minutes of HRDC A.R.P. Committee, 7.3.39.
3. SECH, 25.8.39.
4. SECH, 18.8.39.
5. SECH, 25.8.39 and 6.10.39.
6. ESCC Survey of A.R.P. Services by District, 31.12.39, ESRO, CD Box.
7. SECH, 29.3.40.
8. HRDC Minutes, 2.9.39.
9. *Front Line, op. cit.*
10. *H.A.R.P.,* (Hailsham A.R.P.) magazine, September 1941.
11. Personal interview with Miss N. Knowles.
12. SECH, 25.8.39.
13. SECH, 27.10.39.
14. Message form from SERO to all East Sussex Sub-Controls, 14.5.40. ESRO, CD Box.
15. HRDC Emergency Committee, 24.6.40.
16. SECH, 27.10.39.
17. *Hailsham Parish Magazine,* June 1940.
18. ESCC A.R.P. Inspection Report on HRDC, 17.10.39, ESRO, CD Box and HRDC Emergency Committee Minutes, October 1939 and 20.1.40.
19. HRDC Emergency Committee Minutes, 20.1.40 & 3.2.40 and HRDC Minutes 15.5.40.
20. Hailsham School Log Book, Autumn Term, 1940.
21. HRDC Emergency Committee Minutes, May and June 1940.
22. Written memories of Mr E. Pitcher.
23. *Front Line, op.cit,* and *Greensleeves,* the story of the W.V.S., undated.
24. Miss N. Knowles.
25. *Front Line, op.cit.*
26. Personal interview with Mr S. Salvage, Hailsham A.R.P. worker.
27. SECH, 12.9.49.
28. *Front Line, op.cit.*
29. Personal interview with Mr Salvage.
30. SECH, 19.9.41.
31. Mr S. Salvage.
32. SECH, 10.1.41.
33. SECH, 3.9.41.
34. Mr S. Salvage.
35. Hailsham W.I. Minutes, undated.

36. SECH: various articles in August and September 1939.
37. Mr S. Salvage.
38. SECH, 2.2.41.
39. Sussex 100 File: British Red Cross War Service: Brighton H.Q.
40. Annual Year Book of the British Red Cross War Service (Hailsham) for 1939, pages 46 and 54.
41. Personal interview with Dr H.F. Shaw.
42. Mr Salvage.
43. Personal interview with Mrs M.K. Burgess, Red Cross.
44. Written memories of Mr A.J. Burgess, Order of St John's, wartime Divisional Superintendent.
45. Personal interview with Mr T. Marchant, wartime member of St John's.
46. HRDC, 1.11.40.
47. *Ibid*, 3.1.41.
48. SECH, 5.1.40.
49. ESCC, A.R.P. Incident Book, 1940.
50. Personal interview with Major Batten, wartime member of Hailsham Home Guard and farmer in the Rushlake Green-Cowbeech area.
51. *Ibid*.
52. *Ibid*.
53. Personal interview with Mr J. Roberts.
54. Mr Salvage.
55. Personal interview with Miss Rous.
56. *The War in East Sussex,* compiled by SECH, p.27, undated.

Chapter 5

1. Written information supplied by Mr Faulkner, Hailsham Food Executive Officer.
2. HRDC Minutes, 2.3.39 and SECH, 8.9.39.
3. Written information supplied by Mrs D. Walker, worker at the Hailsham Food Office.
4. *Keep Smiling Through,* Susan Briggs, Weidenfeld and Nicholson.
5. SECH, 5.1.40.
6. SECH, 5.4.40.
7. Hailsham W.I. Minutes, August 1940.
8. SECH, 25.7.41.
9. Mr Faulkner.
10. Written information supplied by Mrs D. White.
11. SECH, various articles and general tone, June 1940 to July 1941.
12. Emergency Powers (Defence), Motor Vehicles, 26.6.40.
13. Written information supplied by Mr E.Pitcher.
14. Personal interview with Major Batton, wartime farmer in the Rushlake Green-Cowbeech area.
15. SECH, 12.1.40.
16. SECH, 4.7.41.
17. SECH, 11.7.41.
18. SECH, 8.9.39 and 15.9.39.
19. SECH, 27.10.39.
20. SECH, 18.8.39.
21. SECH, 12.1.40.
22. SECH, 13.9.40; 20.9.40; 27.9.40.
23. Information supplied by Mr W. Marshall, member of the War Agricultural Committee in the Hailsham area.

24. SECH, 22.9.39 and 27.10.39.
25. Personal interview with Mr Salvage, wartime worker at Knight's Nurseries.
26. Major Batten.
27. SECH, various articles, July and August 1940.
28. HRDC Minutes, 17.6.40.
29. HRDC Minutes, 12.6.40.
30. Information supplied by Miss N. Knowles, Hailsham A.R.P. worker.
31. SECH, 26.12.41.
32. *Sussex County Magazine,* Jan. 1941.
33. SECH, 5.4.40.

Chapter 6

1. *East Sussex Federation of Women's Institutes 1919-1979: a Short History,* Marjorie Steward, published by the East Sussex Federation, 1979.
2. HWIM, April and May 1940, May, June, July 1941.
3. SECH, 7.7.41 and 28.7.41.
4. HWIM, various entries July 1940 to December 1941.
5. HPM, November to March 1939-40.
6. HWIM, September 1939 to July 1940.
7. Information supplied by Mr E. Pitcher.
8. Information supplied by Mrs Hanks.
9. HPM, September 1939.
10. HRDC Minutes, 29.12.39 and SECH, 19.7.40.
11. HWIM, October 1941.
12. HPM, October 1939 and May 1940.
13. Information supplied by Mr E. Pitcher.
14. HRDC Salvage Sub-Committee Minutes, February 1940.
15. SECH, 12.9.41.
16. HRDC Salvage Sub-Committee Minutes, February 1940.
17. SECH, 17.5.40.
18. HRDC Salvage Sub-Committee Minutes, June 1940; and Finance and General Purposes Sub-Committee Minutes, 5.6.40.
19. SECH, 8.9.39.
20. Information supplied by a Hailsham housewife.
21. Information supplied by Mrs D. White.
22. Information supplied by Mrs Mobbs, teacher in charge of London evacuees in Hailsham.
23. SECH, 6.10.39 and 13.10.39.
24. *Ibid,* 6.10.39.
25. HRDC Evacuation Sub-Committee Minutes, early October 1939.
26. Information supplied by Mr H. Maryan, Hailsham Parish Billeting Officer; and Summary of Receipts at Cancellation of Billets, September 15th to September 26th 1939.
27. *The People's War,* Angus Calder, Panther, 1979.
28. Information supplied by Mr H. Maryan.
29. *Ibid* and Hailsham School Admissions Register, September 1939 to September 1940.
30. *Ibid,* May, July, September and November 1940.
31. *Ibid,* January 1941.

Chapter 7

1. Information supplied by Captain R. Baker.
2. Information supplied by Major O.A. Batten.
3. Information supplied by Mr F. Clark, Hailsham A.R.P. worker.
4. Information supplied by Mrs M.K. Burgess.
5. Information supplied by a Hailsham housewife.
6. Information supplied by Mrs D. White.
7. SCM, November 1941.
8. SECH, Feb. 1964; also undated article in 1975.
9. SCM, November 1940.
10. SCM, November 1943.

ABBREVIATIONS

ESRO: East Sussex Record Office
CD: Civil Defence
LDV: Local Defence Volunteers
SERO: South Eastern Regional Office (Regional Civil Defence Commissioner)
HRDC: Hailsham Rural District Council
SCM: Sussex County Magazine
SECH: Sussex Express and County Herald
HWIM: Hailsham W.I. Minutes
HPM: Hailsham Parish Magazine
HG: Home Guard
ESCC: East Sussex County Council